The C Zone

The C Zone

PEAK PERFORMANCE UNDER PRESSURE

Robert J. Kriegel, Ph.D.
and Marilyn Harris Kriegel, Ph.D.

ANCHOR PRESS/DOUBLEDAY
GARDEN CITY, NEW YORK
1984

Library of Congress Cataloging in Publication Data

Kriegel, Robert.
  The C zone.

  1. Stress (Psychology) 2. Performance—Psychological
aspects. 3. Exercise therapy. I. Kriegel, Marilyn
Harris. II. Title.
BF575.S75K74   1984   158'.1

ISBN: 0-385-18771-8
Library of Congress Catalog Card Number 84-48707

This book is dedicated with love and respect
to Edith K. Kriegel and Myrtle H. Harris.

ABOUT THE AUTHORS

Psychologist **Robert J. Kriegel**, Ph. D., is a former All-American athlete who was an advertising executive with Young and Rubicam before he left to become one of the early figures in the human potential movement. In addition to leading seminars for the Esalen Institute, he founded and directed Esalen's Consulting Service, which designed and conducted management training programs for such organizations as the U.S. Army, Model Cities, Cal Trans and Memorex. He developed and directed the Esalen Sports Center, which, according to the New York *Times*, "spurred a sporting revolution in human performance practices."

In 1977, with Tim Gallwey, he wrote the bestselling *Inner Skiing* and directed the highly acclaimed Inner Skiing programs that were conducted throughout the United States and Europe.

Dr. Kriegel has also designed and conducted seminars on optimal performance, stress management, fitness and wellness for such clients as AT&T, CBS, Levi Strauss, Syntex, the Ford Foundation and the U.S. Forest Service, among others. He has been adjunct faculty at the University of San Francisco and at Antioch University's Graduate Center for Holistic Studies, and is an advisory board member of the California Governor's Council on Wellness and Physical Fitness. In addition, he has been the "mental coach" for many professional, Olympic and world-class athletes.

Dr. **Marilyn Harris Kriegel** has designed and taught programs in thinking, creativity, counseling and communication for professional training institutes, colleges and universities in both the United States and Europe. Most recently she was the cochair of Antioch University West's graduate psychology program in holistic studies. She has also served on the faculty of Dominican College, Hebrew Union College in Los Angeles and Goddard College.

Dr. Kriegel was a founder of Seminars for Women, an organization that developed programs on commitment, risk-taking and the achievement of goals for women executives and entrepreneurs. She was also the director of a three-year federally funded project in curriculum development and teacher training in the Newark, California, public schools, as well as the associate director of education at Esalen Institute and the director of professional training at Anthos Institute in New York.

Dr. Kriegel is a licensed marriage, family and child counselor and maintains a private practice.

ACKNOWLEDGMENTS

Our friend Anne Herbert wisely suggested that books should be published with a masthead like magazines and newspapers. We agree. They are rarely the work of one mind or heart. The following is the masthead for this book: people to whom we are deeply grateful for their assistance, encouragement and loving support.

—Gail Kriegel for her keen writer's mind and sharp editor's pencil which had a major impact on the book. Gail inspired and encouraged us throughout and showed us how to work together on this project.
—Curt Berrien, Richard Leifer, Mark Rosenblatt, Kristin Shannon, Deborah Ward and Linda Weinreb for their thoughtful and valuable feedback on the work in progress.
—Kay Goldstein and JeanA Warner for their willingness to work odd hours and last minutes.

—Rik Jadricek for making our computer "user-friendly" and us computer-literate.

—Dr. Frank "Zeke" McCord for his assistance constructing the Performance Zone Profile and his great sports stories.

—Jay George for his enthusiasm and help in organizing the test scores and footnotes.

—John Brockman, our agent, for his sound advice and support.

—Peyton Moss, our editor at Doubleday, for his clear editing, terrific ideas, endless availability and overall Type C attitude.

—Phil Pochoda at Doubleday for his interest and enthusiasm for the project.

—Sara Alexander, David Brandt, Laurie Brandt, Ken Dychtwald and Naomi Remen for their suggestions, love and support.

—All of the people who have attended our seminars over the past twenty years whose participation helped us learn about the C Zone.

—To all of the peak performers who took the time to be interviewed and were frank enough to share some of themselves with us.

—Otis Kriegel for his understanding of our late-night and weekend work sessions, his thoughtful suggestions, which were far beyond what we had thought to be an eleven-year-old's experience and understanding. For his enthusiastic support, his many hugs and the spark and humor and love he provides to our home and office.

AUTHORS' NOTE

Because this book is co-authored yet written in the first person, we thought an explanation was necessary to avoid confusion. The book represents our combined forty years' experience working with peak performers and teaching people to perform at their best. The collaboration was a true C Zone experience, combining commitment, communication and cooperation, one filled with joy as well as sweat, heart as well as mind.

In writing this book we had to practice its precepts. Progress was only possible when both of us were able to let go of our attachments to "mine" and to allow our talents to cooperate creatively. Sometimes when the first person is used it clearly refers to one of us. At other times we felt the distinction was not important.

Also, because the English language does not have a word for third-person singular that does not connote gender we attempted to use "he" and "she" equally.

Until one is committed, there is hesitancy, the chance to draw back, always ineffectiveness, concerning all acts of initiative (and creation). There is one elementary truth the ignorance of which kills countless ideas and splendid plans: that the moment one definitely commits oneself, then providence moves too. All sorts of things occur to help one that would never otherwise have occurred. A whole stream of events issues from the decision, raising in one's favour all manner of unforeseen incidents and meetings and material assistance which no man could have dreamed would have come his way. Whatever you can do or dream you can, begin it. Boldness has genius, power and magic in it. Begin it now.

GOETHE

CONTENTS

INTRODUCTION

Type C Behavior: Performance under Pressure

Pressure's the name of the game today. Not just the pressure to get ahead but the stress of trying to make it in a world where every time you look up the rules of the game have changed. There's good reason we feel pressured. The world around us is becoming more competitive and less predictable with each passing day. In the past forty years the human race has entered the atomic age, the space age and the computer age.[1]

Today's pace and the struggle to earn a living and get ahead places tough new demands on us: Not only does the average American change jobs every three years but people entering the work force will have to understand twenty-four times as much information as they would have a generation ago. Most management personnel will soon spend 60 percent of their time learning new information, leaving only 40 percent to get the actual job done.

Type A Behavior

A common response to the pressure caused by this growth of information and acceleration of change is to try and SPEED UP. The harried individual trying to keep up with these changes talks fast, walks fast and acts as if slowing down to relax is tantamount to failure. Life is a continual race against the clock.

Cardiologists Ray Rosenman and Meyer Friedman labeled this supercharged behavior Type A. Time is the Type A's enemy. There is a sense of urgency about everything he does. He gets extremely agitated when anyone takes "too long" to do a job, come up with an answer or even complete a sentence.

Although some Type A's do perform well under the gun and claim they like the pressure, they pay a price. Their "struggle with the clock is a never-ending exercise in futility. . . . The time pressures leave them frustrated, nervous, hostile . . . "[2] As if that were not bad enough, Rosenman and Friedman found that these types were three times more likely to develop heart diseases than their less driven colleagues. The research also found that they are more susceptible to burnout and all of the other diseases that come from high stress.

The irony is that while many Type A's use achievement to justify their behavior, they don't perform nearly as well as they could. They become hyperactive, and rush around trying to do too much, too quickly, and as a result accomplish little of quality.

Type B Behavior

Standing patiently on line at the opposite end of Rosenman and Friedman's spectrum is the Type B. This type is characterized as low-key, non-competitive and free of the sense of urgency associated with the Type A.

But though the Type B may be more desirable from a health perspective, there is something missing. Call it spark, fire or vigor. Type B's lack the excitement, enthusiasm and dynamism needed to perform at peak levels under pressure. They don't seem to confront the challenges or take the risks necessary for big rewards. (To find eighty men who fitted the description of a Type B, the two cardiologists had to go to the municipal clerks' and the embalmers' unions.)

A New Model

Are there only A's or B's? Is the choice to be heart-attack-prone and achievement-driven or tweedy, thoughtful and living in the country? Is Type B a realistic alternative when we need to respond quickly and appropriately to a world that is constantly changing even though we'd like it to stand still? The two styles are clearly insufficient as performance models for the pressures of the 1980s work world. Where is the model for performing at peak levels under pressure without the debilitating effects of stress?

The descriptions of Types A and B also leave out the moments of excellence and peak performance under pressure that all of us have had and which characterize top performers in all fields.

What are these moments of excellence? Are they accidents? Can they be repeated? Why do they occur? Can we feel that way more often? Are top performers just born into a class of their own or do they know and do something we don't?

This book answers these questions and uncovers a new model for high performance, Type C behavior. Type C is

peak performance under pressure without the debilitating effects of stress that rob us of our health and enjoy-
ment of life. Type C provides a model for continued
growth and learning and for living life under pressure
with vitality, meaning and joy. Learning to perform as a
Type C enables you to uncover and express your innate
potential and use it to perform optimally—no matter
what the external pressure.

Type C behavior is a performance model for us all.
Everyone, as the book demonstrates, can perform as a
Type C. Whether you're directing a multibillion-dollar
corporation or managing a small office, selling or speaking, running a machine or running for election, marketing
or manufacturing, teaching or training, researching or
reporting, out looking for a first job or wanting to change
careers—WHATEVER YOU DO, YOU CAN DO IT
AS A TYPE C.

Type C behavior will help you increase your effectiveness and accomplish your goals more easily in this increas-
ingly high-pressure climate, no matter what you do or
where you do it.

High-Pressure Performers

We began to document Type C behavior in 1970 when I
was directing the Esalen Institute Sports Center. There
we worked with world-class athletes to determine the
mental factors that shape maximum performance.

World-class athletes are perhaps the most visible high-
pressure performers in our culture today. Imagine how
you'd feel if every time you made a decision you had to
face a stadium filled with people who heckled your every
mistake, and the results of your efforts were published in
the morning papers.

The ability of these men and women to handle incredible pressure is what determines whether they will succeed or not. Baseball Hall of Fame pitching great Christy Mathewson said, "It's in the clutch that you show whether or not you are a big-leaguer. Pressure is the acid test. That's the reason that so many who shine in the minor leagues fail to make good in the major leagues. They cannot stand the fire."[3]

One result of our work with these athletes at the Sports Center was a national symposium on the mental aspects of high performance, which, as the New York *Times* headlined, "Spurred a Sporting Revolution."

Sports and Business: High-Pressure Arenas

When Timothy Gallwey and I wrote *Inner Skiing*, we were very gratified by how well it was received. This book presented a new way to think about skiing. But I am convinced that another reason it spent so many months on the New York *Times* bestseller list was that readers found that they could apply its techniques to other things besides sports. In fact, an unexpected benefit of conducting sports seminars for coaches and "weekend" athletes throughout North America and Europe was the discovery that the same techniques that worked so well to improve performance in sport, worked equally well to improve performance at work.

This connection led Marilyn and me to develop and conduct programs on "Peak Performance under Pressure" for a wide range of corporations, government agencies, universities and hospitals. Although the participants were not athletes, they were interested in maximizing their performance at work. Participants in these programs learn techniques used by world-class athletes to master stressful situations, remain calm under pressure, improve concentration, learn new skills, overcome slumps, increase motivation and perform more consistently at peak levels.

As we moved between the locker room and the board room we found specific characteristics that are common to all high performers regardless of their field. To sharpen the definition of these high-performance characteristics, we conducted a research study that included personal interviews with over 400 executives. We also reviewed questionnaires from peak performers in a variety of fields, ranging from the chief executive officer of a Fortune 100 corporation, to the doctor voted most valuable professor at a major medical school, to an individual who turned a recipe for a natural-food cake mix into a nationally distributed product. The results of this study, along with our experience conducting hundreds of seminars in sports, business, and education and my work with world-class athletes, became the basis for the high-performance Type C model and techniques discussed in this book.

This research and field work showed that we don't have to react to pressure by being driven and aggressive Type A's or patient and passive Type B's.

Type C's, those who perform at their peak under pressure, choose the behavior most suited to their needs. These peak performers all demonstrated three consistent characteristics: commitment, confidence and control. Learning to increase and integrate each of these Type C characteristics is one of the main focuses of this book.

The High-Performance Formula

To perform as a Type C in any field requires a combination of specific skills and attitudes.

Skill includes a thorough knowledge of whatever game you are playing; the ability to develop game-winning strategies that capitalize on your strengths; and a basic competence or expertise in the execution phase of your profession, whether it be hitting a top-spin backhand or managing a business.

We use the term "attitude" to include all of our "inner" or mental processes, many of which are unconscious. Attitude incorporates your self-image; what you believe or imagine will happen in an upcoming situation; what you think and how you feel now.

The effect your level of skill has on your performance is obvious. The effect of your attitude on your performance is more subtle, but telling under pressure. Your attitude not only determines how well you execute your skills or express what you know; it also determines how often you will perform as a Type C.

An example of the effect attitude has on performance is how much better you do in practice when you are loose and relaxed than you often do in a real game when you're under pressure. The tightness and tension that prevents you from performing up to and beyond your already demonstrated ability level when under pressure, is caused by your attitude.

Fear of failure, lack of confidence, weak motivation and unrealistic expectations block your innate Type C potential and prevent it from being expressed. Until you learn to master these "mental" obstacles you'll never be a top performer no matter how skilled you are. You'll always leave your game on the practice court.

A Type C attitude, which combines confidence, commitment and control, will help you overcome seemingly insurmountable obstacles and transcend your level of skill. Baseball great Pete Rose, nicknamed "Charlie Hustle," doesn't have the same natural ability as many of his peers, but he is the second most prolific hitter in baseball history. Ty Cobb, the one man who has more hits than Rose, was the same type of player: one whose confidence and burning desire more than made up for any lack of skill.

Speaking of the highly technical sport of slalom ski racing, in which a racer is constantly being challenged by new techniques and equipment, Olympic gold medalist and three-time World Cup winner Phil Mahre says, "The most vital aspect of winning is mental attitude."[4]

"Mental attitude," former Stanford All-American quarterback Guy Benjamin believes, "is what separates the 10 to 20 percent who are going to be stars, no matter what, from the rest of us."[5]

A recent nationwide cross-industry study, conducted by the Forum Corporation, found that the most significant factor that distinguished top from moderate performers was attitude.[6]

The high-performing executives we interviewed substantiated the findings of the Forum Corporation's study. Although each expressed it differently, over 90 percent of those we interviewed said it was their attitude, not their intelligence or skills, that made the difference.

Tony Morgan, who grew up in modest surroundings in England, went on to win an Olympic silver medal in sailing, and became an extremely successful international businessman, and a Governor of the British Broadcasting Corporation. When asked to what he attributed his success, Morgan laughed. "I really don't know. I am no smarter than the next guy. I'd have to guess it was my attitude that got me where I am. I think I wanted it more than the next guy and was willing to work harder and take the necessary risks."

Although many people would agree that high performance is a combination of skill and attitude, the main emphasis in traditional training programs so far has been on the acquisition of skills and knowledge. Attitude training, the other half of the high-performance formula, is given only lip service.

The common belief is that attitude can't be learned. "You've either got it or you don't." All the Type C athletes and business people whom we interviewed and worked with prove otherwise.

The Type C

The ability to perform as a Type C is innate in everyone. Behind the doubts, fears and other mental obstacles is the potential to perform as a C in whatever you are doing.

This book can serve as a training manual to enable you to enhance your Type C characteristics and master the mental obstacles that are preventing you from performing as a C more often. Learning, practicing and mastering these Type C skills will help you to expand your options, transcend your limits and perform consistently at your peak under pressure.

The C Zone

CHAPTER ONE

The Type C Experience

Have you ever had one of those days when everything you did worked? Things just seemed to fall into place. You were more productive with less effort and completely in tune with what you were doing. You felt great, on top of everything.

That's a Type C experience. It's a high-performance episode in which you transcend your normal level of ability. Type C behavior enables you to perform at your peak whatever the situation. And although you are more effective at these times, it feels as if you aren't working nearly so hard as usual, for you are vital and full of energy.

"It's like being on a roll," says Congresswoman Barbara Boxer. "I feel confident and enthusiastic and everything seems to work. I am able to accomplish a great deal with a minimum of effort. My energy keeps building and gets transferred to whomever I am working with."

"I seem to be able to stay relaxed in what would ordinarily be very tense meetings," said Tom Simpson, who became president of Norwegian Caribbean Lines at thirty-three and doubled their revenues to $100 million within three years. "I feel as if I am not trying as hard as usual and yet I am much more effective."

Emmy Award-winning TV news reporter Doug Kriegel says, "Sometimes when I'm rushing to meet a deadline, I become so involved in what I am doing that I am unaware of anything going on around me. I get calm and everything becomes easy. It's unbelievable. I've done my best work at these times."

The qualities most inherent in a Type C episode are those you experience and associate with doing your best. A Type C experience is:

Transcendent. You are much more effective and productive than usual. You break your own records.

Effortless. You perform better without "trying hard", or straining. Whatever you do seems easier than usual.

Positive. You are optimistic. You have confidence. You feel good about yourself and what you are doing.

Spontaneous. You feel as if there is a natural flow between your thoughts and actions. Your humor is evident. Choices come easily and automatically.

Focused. Your concentration is intense. You feel totally involved in your work, connected to what you are doing and to the people you are working with.

Vital. You experience high energy, which gives you a feeling of joy and well-being. You feel healthier and more alive.

Type C behavior isn't restricted to superstars or superachievers. Everyone has performed at the Type C level at some point. This high-performance behavior can be expressed in any number of ways: receptiveness when learning a new skill; aggressiveness and daring when confronting a challenge; energy and expansiveness when talking to a large group. It can produce the extra energy needed for handling a sudden overload situation; the presence of mind to give each call your full attention when all the buttons on your phone are blinking; or the intense concentration and concern for detail you need when preparing a complex report.

The Three C's: Synergy in Action

Confidence, commitment and *control* are the characteristics most frequently mentioned by people describing their Type C experiences. These three Type C characteristics are inherent in everyone, though developed to different degrees. But Type C behavior is not a result of any single one of these attitudinal factors. It is determined by the interrelationship of all three.

When you are confident about what you are doing, strongly committed to it and in control of yourself and your actions, synergy occurs. The resulting Type C behavior is more than the sum of each of these individual characteristics. When the musicians in an orchestra are playing in perfect harmony, the result is a symphony that transcends the sum of the sounds of each instrument. No one characteristic is more important than another when performing at Type C levels. Your confidence, commitment and control, like the instruments of an orchestra, are working in harmony with each other to make whatever you are doing seem like beautiful music.

Type C Behavior: Choice or Chance?

Joan A., the marketing manager for a consumer packaged goods company, told of a Type C experience she had in her first budget meeting with the vice-president of finance for her company. "I had to present my yearly plans and operating budget to him and I heard he was real tough. A strictly 'by the numbers' person, and I had a lot of conjecture in my marketing plan. I was in a cold sweat and hadn't slept much the night before. The topper was that when I got to the meeting the president of the company was there as well as the vice-president of marketing. Since it was a major product introduction they told me they all wanted to be in on the plans. Normally I would have been panicked. I'm not real good at making presentations at the best of times and I almost had a heart attack when I saw them all sitting there.

"But for some reason I felt calm when I started talking. I wasn't intimidated as I normally would have been. I seemed to know their concerns before they voiced them and had the perfect answer out of my mouth without even thinking about it. I was amazed at how I was responding to their questions; I sounded so confident. When I left the office, I was floating. I not only got what I asked for but they told me they were so impressed with my plans that they gave me a 10 percent increase in my budget request. If I could be like that in every meeting I'd be the hottest executive in town."

When we asked Joan A. why she thought she had a Type C episode during this budget meeting, she shrugged her shoulders. "I don't know. I was well prepared but I'm always well prepared for meetings, especially important ones like that one. Usually I get very intimidated in pressure situations. But for some reason—I still can't figure it out—I was really 'on' for that meeting. It just seemed to happen."

For many people, like Joan, Type C episodes happen by chance. For no apparent reason you suddenly get hot in a tennis match and play way over your head. Or "out of nowhere" the work you have been struggling to get finished just starts flowing. Sometimes this experience occurs when you have prepared well and are feeling confident; sometimes when you are feeling down or tense. Yet in both cases the Type C episode seems to happen by accident. So people attribute their Type C performance to luck and return to operating the way they usually do, hoping that luck will come their way again.

A Type C episode isn't a rare peak experience that comes once in a lifetime, when you get lucky. It isn't some far-off nirvana that may be reached by meditating for hours at a time and forsaking all other endeavors. It is a high plateau of optimal-performance behavior that you have already experienced and that you can reach over and over again. These experiences of high performance can be reached repeatedly and sustained for longer periods of time because they are reflective of our innate ability. But this natural high-performance state is usually blocked by bad habits, unexamined fears and a lack of familiarity with and acceptance of the Type C that lies dormant and unrecognized within us.

Of course, no one performs at Type C levels all the time. Even Chris Evert Lloyd, once dubbed the "ice queen" for her unflappability under pressure, chokes in an important match now and then. Even the "Golden Bear," Jack Nicklaus, perhaps the finest golfer ever, sometimes blows an easy putt. But one difference between peak performers like these and everyone else is that they have Type C episodes more often and for longer periods of time than most people. The frequency, duration and intensity of their C episodes are greater because they have learned how to make them happen intentionally. They have developed methods that evoke this desired state when they need it. *With most people Type C episodes happen by chance; with most peak performers they happen by choice.*

The techniques outlined in this book will help you to

learn how to make Type C episodes happen more often and when you really need them. Type C episodes will still happen to you by chance when you least expect them; however, the more you practice these techniques, the easier it will be for you to make your Type C episodes happen when and where you want them to—by choice rather than by chance. As the great golfer Ben Hogan once said, "The more you practice, the luckier you get."

Increasing Type C Behavior

Type C behavior isn't the province of a chosen few. We all have and can use this incredible power to go just about anywhere we want to go. Some of us are constantly making the most of this power while in others this vast potential goes largely untapped. But it is there and waiting to be used.

Nobel Prize winner Albert Szent-Györgyi pointed out that all human beings have a natural tendency to expand and make the most of their potential.[1] To do more and be more is the goal toward which Type C strives. It means tapping into the latent potential that exists within each one of us and using that power to experience and express ourselves more fully.

Type C Experience

1. Recall and describe in detail a Type C episode that you had.
2. What were you feeling at that time?
3. What was going on in your mind?
4. What was the experience like physically?
5. What were the qualities that you expressed at these times? (E.g., confidence, courage, power, poise, charisma.)
6. Get up and walk around. Allow yourself to feel the way

you did then. Let your posture, your walk, everything you do, reflect your Type C experience.

7. Imagine answering the phone as a Type C.

Imagine writing your next memo or letter as a Type C.

Imagine making a Type C presentation in your next meeting.

Imagine negotiating as a Type C.

Imagine disagreeing with your boss as a Type C.

Make a note of the qualities you bring to each task when you are expressing your innate Type C attitude.

CHAPTER TWO

Operating in the C Zone

Top athletes commonly refer to their high-performance episodes as "playing in the zone." But the zones we play in aren't always peak-performance zones. There are actually three performance zones—the C Zone, the Panic Zone and the Drone Zone. Each encompasses a different type of behavior.

The C Zone: From Mastery to Challenge

When in your C Zone you are constantly shuttling back and forth between mastery and challenge. Mastery is achieving competency or expertise at what you are doing. Challenge is upping the ante and playing for higher stakes by taking the risks that are necessary to get you to the next level. This mastery/challenge shuttle is a natural Type C process through which you learn and grow in everything you do throughout your life.

Moving from mastery to challenge is like climbing a

ladder, not an unfamiliar metaphor for achieving success. In this ascent toward the top, mastery, the achievement of competency, provides you with a strong footing and a solid base. Mastery involves remaining on a rung until you have gotten your balance and feel confident, comfortable and in control. The challenge comes when you commit yourself to taking the risk of moving up to a higher step. Initially you feel shaky at this new height. At this point you strive for mastery, to gain balance and confidence, until you are once again ready for the next challenge. The mastery/challenge shuttle, as can be seen in the diagram, takes you from the excitement of exploring the unknown to the satisfaction and fulfillment of a job well done. It shuttles you from uncertainty to certainty and back, keeps you learning, growing and moving up the ladder.

The late Dr. Willie Unsoeld, the first American to reach the summit of Everest, once told me, "You need an element of risk, a challenge to perform at your peak. The right amount of risk throws you into a state of total concentration where there is nothing but the moment. You feel as if you have more time and more strength to accomplish things than you ever thought possible. But before you take that risk you've got to master the fundamentals and become competent in the technical aspects of what it is you are doing."

Describing this mastery/challenge shuttle, Tom Simpson told us, "I love challenging myself. There's a certain tension when you are on your edge that is exquisite. I feel drawn to the front lines. However, before I put myself out there, I always try to know as much as possible about what I am doing."

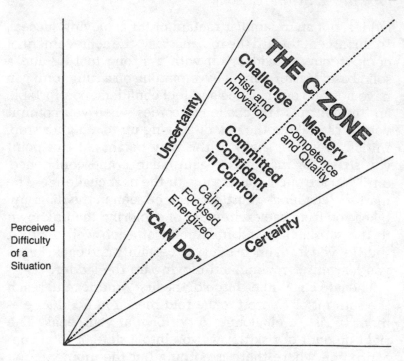

Perceived Ability to Handle Situation

Reexperiencing Challenge and Mastery

We have all experienced both the challenge and the mastery of the C Zone.

Challenge

Take a moment and reflect on several times in your life when you challenged yourself and took a risk in any area of endeavor. Remember the excitement and anticipation of trying something that was new, uncertain and a little out of your control. Remember how it felt—the energy, the fear, how vital and alive you were feeling, how your concentration sharpened and everything was experienced with more intensity.

Make a list of some of the risks you've taken. As you list them, remember them in as much detail as you can. Reexperience the challenge as fully as you can.

Now make another list of several challenges that you would like to take in the future, areas in which you are considering taking a risk.

Mastery

Take a moment and remember several aspects of your life in which you have achieved mastery. Reflect on the feeling of satisfaction that you derived from doing something well. Experience the ease and confidence with which you go about this work.

List several areas in your life in which you have achieved mastery, become competent or expert. Once again as you write each down, reflect on how it feels to note your accomplishment.

Now list a few areas in your life in which you would like to develop more competence and expertise.

Creativity and Spontaneity

The C Zone shuttle between mastery and challenge is a vehicle not only for growth and improvement but for creativity and spontaneity as well.

Top speakers, those who interact spontaneously with their audiences; salespeople who adapt a presentation on the spur of the moment; supervisors and managers who must respond instantaneously to a wide range of problems; anyone who thinks creatively on his feet—all have in common mastery of their material. Mastery frees each of them to accept the challenge of the moment and to respond spontaneously, often with a surprising creativity.

Victor Borge is a perfect example of the spontaneity that results from mastery. Taking random suggestions from an audience, he plays current pop tunes as they might have been played by Mozart, Beethoven and other great composers. Underlying Borge's amazing spontaneity, however, is his mastery of the subjects.

Basketball star Julius Erving, the inimitable Dr. J., believes that "unless you dare to put yourself at center stage and dare to be great, you never will."[1] But Dr. J. also adds that for every move of his on the court that looks spontaneous and daring, he has spent hours practicing in the gym.

Out of Your C Zone

We have all experienced the shuttle from mastery to challenge and back that characterizes Type C behavior. Most of us, however, gravitate toward either challenge or mastery. Some people devote most of their energies to honing their skills or increasing competence in one area. They enjoy mastery and control. Others are drawn more to the excitement of a challenge. They love to take risks and explore new territories.

But the person who is always overcommitting, continually taking risks and challenging herself, is like the skier who constantly takes slopes that are a little too difficult. Sure it's exciting, but if you never take the time to master the fundamentals, sooner or later you'll take one risk too many and end up in your Panic Zone.

On the other hand, if you concentrate solely on increasing control and mastering the finer points of a task, you'll eventually come to a place of diminishing returns. The skier who has the ability to move up a level, but continues to ski the same slopes, will stop improving. Eventually he will lose his enthusiasm, become lethargic and end up in his Drone Zone.

The Panic Zone

Because they are highly motivated, many people in our results-oriented society overcommit and overchallenge themselves. They take on too many responsibilities or inordinately high risks and get in over their heads and out of control. Trying too hard to do too much in too little time, they drive themselves into their Panic Zone.

In the Panic Zone you experience great bursts of energy. But that energy is fueled by panic. You are out of control. Your concentration darts from one thought to another with the speed of a strobe light, causing you to race around frantically and fruitlessly.

The experience is like playing tennis with someone who is much better than you are but whom you desperately want to beat. You scramble from one side of the court to the other to retrieve a shot, your adrenaline pumping, your heart beating wildly. Then before you can catch your breath, your opponent hits it to the other side of the court. You race over, just manage to return it, and she hits it well out of your reach again. And off you go . . .

When in your Panic Zone, you're not in control of a situation, but reacting to it. You have no time to plan, to develop creative strategies, to problem-solve effectively or to master any skill. All of your energy is wasted racing to get that ball that is always out of reach, or to accomplish the task that is more than you can handle.

An excellent example of being in the Panic Zone is Type A behavior. Time is the enemy of Type A's. They hate waiting. They get impatient and irritable when any-

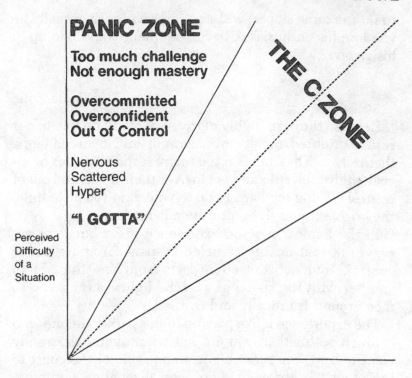

PANIC ZONE

Too much challenge
Not enough mastery

Overcommitted
Overconfident
Out of Control

Nervous
Scattered
Hyper

"I GOTTA"

Perceived
Difficulty
of a
Situation

THE C ZONE

Perceived Ability to Handle Situation

one takes too long to complete a job, answer a question or even finish a sentence.

Dr. Kenneth Pelletier, a leading authority on stress in the workplace, says, "The time pressures inevitably leave [the Type A person] frustrated, nervous, hostile, and even more firmly determined to step up his efforts to accomplish more in less time. His struggle with the clock is a never-ending exercise in futility."[2]

The irony of being in your Panic Zone is that although you use achievement as a justification for this behavior, you usually don't achieve nearly what you are capable of. Dr. Pelletier amplifies: "In his eagerness to get things done as fast as possible, this person may respond to challenges in a rote manner, causing him to make errors in judgment. And since he never takes time to consider new approaches to, or implications of, a situation, his creativity will be inhibited."[3]

Though it may be hard to measure the actual cost in terms of performance, when you are in the Panic Zone it's not hard to measure the cost of this type of behavior to life itself. Friedman and Rosenman concluded that this type is three times as likely to develop heart disease as their less driven colleagues. Panic Zone behavior often results in the stress-related diseases that are now recognized as the major cause of mental and physical illness, premature aging and death in our culture.

The Drone Zone

On the opposite end of the C Zone is the Zone of the Drone. Drawn to mastery, the Drone becomes very competent at what he is doing but never risks losing control by taking the next step. Because of the lack of challenge, his job becomes predictable, routine and dull and he loses interest in it. The Drone Zoner has ample skills to handle the task, but his lethargic attitude causes him to perform poorly.

Jonathan L. was a family counselor for one of the big public utilities in the Southwest. "When I first started this job, I loved it, and couldn't wait to get to work in the morning. The work was fascinating and challenging. But I've been doing it for three years now, and I'm bored. It's the same old routine day in and day out. It gets so I can't tell one person from the next anymore. And what's worse, I don't care. I know that I'm not doing as good a job as I used to. I feel like I'm on automatic. I can't get out of my

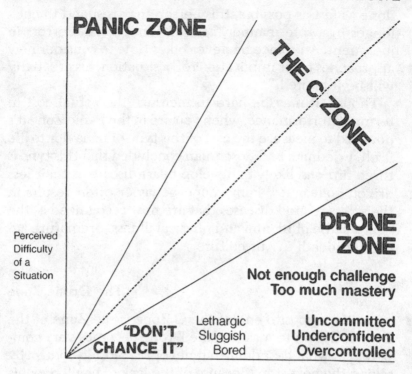

Perceived Ability to Handle Situation

office fast enough at the end of the day. I know it's terrible, but I don't know what to do."

Drone Zoners want to progress and make a move because they are bored and often hate what they are doing. But the fear of failing at the next level prevents them from taking a risk. So they remain where they are, safe but sorry. "I'd like to open my own office," Jonathan continued, "and I know I'm good enough, but it takes a while to get started and develop a good practice. And there's no guarantee that I'll succeed. I've gotten used to making good money here. I'd hate to give that up for something that I'm not sure will work out. I feel stuck."

The Drone Zone may be safe, but it's not free of stress. It's a different kind of stress from that experienced in the Panic Zone. When there don't seem to be any options, you become frustrated and depressed. This kind of negative stress is just as dangerous to your health and well-being as Panic Zone stress. It results in disappointment and many of the depression-based illnesses.

Controlled Stress: A Positive Force

Any discussion of the characteristics of performance would be incomplete without mentioning stress in more detail. Although there is high stress in all three of the performance zones, stress isn't always an enemy. Many recent studies have found that stress is, in fact, important and productive. The crucial distinction is that in your C Zone stress is controlled.

Lack of control is the reason that stress is negative in both the Panic Zone and the Drone Zone. The Panic Zoner is out of control, running around frantically trying to do too much in too little time. The Drone Zoner may have control of his job, but his life is out of control. In spite of his mastery he is stuck. Afraid to challenge himself further, he remains in a situation that he has outgrown.

"According to the latest research," writes award-winning health reporter Susan Seliger, "bad stress is triggered . . . by the feeling that one's decisions are useless, that life is overwhelming and beyond personal control." Positive stress, says Seliger, "comes from rising to challenges, feeling confidence and a sense of control over one's destiny. The ability to control stress is within each person's power. A person who feels in control of his life can channel the stressful energy . . . and make himself healthier. Those people making decisions, the high-powered, high-pressure executives that many have believed are most vulnerable, turn out not to be. And it is not that they are genetically more fit to cope that accounts for their rise to the top. It is their attitude."[4]

"I experience a great deal of stress in both sports and business," Ken Casey, a former professional soccer player and now a general partner in the Professional Investors Security Fund, told us. "But this kind of stress helps me to be more effective. It gives me energy. It's like a pressure cooker. I let it build until just the right time and then take off the cover and turn that stress into action. If you take the cover off too soon, you dissipate all that energy; too late and you dissipate yourself. The key is having that energy under control."

Controlled stress is a source of the energy needed to perform at peak levels in the C Zone. You will learn how to tap into your C Zone capacity for controlling stress in later chapters.

Getting to the C Zone

No one remains in one zone all the time. We move from one to another, sometimes with amazing speed. You may even operate in the Panic Zone in one area of your life and the Drone or C Zone in another. We do, however, tend to favor one zone more. Our personalities gravitate toward challenge and the Panic Zone or mastery and the Drone Zone.

The first thing to do to uncover your own C Zone potential is to learn whether you tend to favor mastery or challenge and to what extent. The Performance Zone Profile in the next chapter will help you recognize your Type C strengths and weaknesses and the zone in which you tend to operate. This information will aid in developing strategies for unblocking your innate Type C abilities so that you will stay in your C Zone more often and for longer periods of time.

Using the Zone Diagram

You can use the Performance Zone Diagram to determine the zone in which you will operate for a specific task.

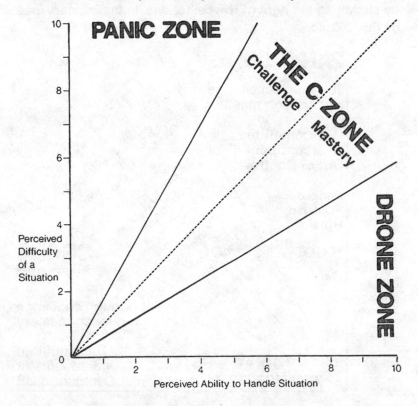

First, mentally rate the difficulty of your task on a scale of 1–10. Try to be as objective as possible. Draw a horizontal line across the diagram at the level you have chosen. Next, rate your ability, on the same 1–10 scale. Draw a vertical line from the point you have chosen. The spot where the two lines intersect will indicate which zone you *expect* to play in during that particular task. If you are taking a risk or challenging yourself, your performance point should be slightly to the left of the center line, in the challenge area of the C Zone. If, on the other hand, you are performing a job in which you need competence and expertise, you should end up slightly to the right of the center line, in the mastery area of the C Zone.

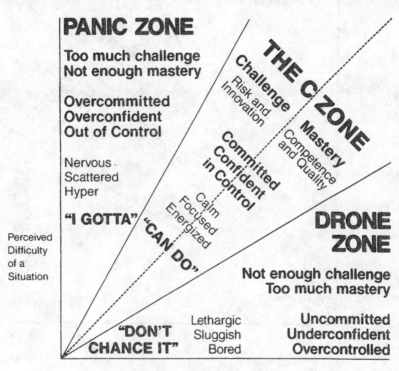

CHAPTER THREE

Type C:
Performance Zone Profile

To determine your predominant performance zone, we have developed a short diagnostic test. You will need about a half hour to take and score your Performance Zone Profile.

Your test score will indicate your C strengths and weaknesses, as well as the performance zone you favor. This information will enable you to identify more easily, and subsequently overcome, the obstacles to your C Zone performance.

Taking the Test

Focus on your performance at work. Answer each question honestly. Circle the number that most accurately describes your behavior as it actually is, not as you would like it to be or think it should be. Telling it like it is will

give you the most reliable feedback and make the test
results accurate and useful.

Type C Performance Zone Profile

**SCORING: 1 IS TOTAL DISAGREEMENT. 7 IS TOTAL
AGREEMENT.**

1. I can do anything I try.
   1 2 3 4 5 6 7
2. I am constantly in over my head.
   1 2 3 4 5 6 7
3. I'll try anything once.
   1 2 3 4 5 6 7
4. I am an overachiever.
   1 2 3 4 5 6 7
5. I don't like to try something I am unsure of.
   1 2 3 4 5 6 7
6. I often get so involved I lose track of time.
   1 2 3 4 5 6 7
7. I'll do anything to achieve my goals.
   1 2 3 4 5 6 7
8. I seek challenges.
   1 2 3 4 5 6 7
9. I have a hard time pulling out of it when I fail.
   1 2 3 4 5 6 7
10. I am cautious in my acceptance of new ideas.
    1 2 3 4 5 6 7
11. My work is my life.
    1 2 3 4 5 6 7
12. I am a stickler for details.
    1 2 3 4 5 6 7
13. I play it safe.
    1 2 3 4 5 6 7
14. I feel as if I have to constantly prove myself.

1 2 3 4 5 6 7

15. I want to be the best at what I do.

1 2 3 4 5 6 7

16. I'd rather be safe than sorry.

1 2 3 4 5 6 7

17. I don't spend enough time preparing for important events.

1 2 3 4 5 6 7

18. I'm a hard driver.

1 2 3 4 5 6 7

19. I have a dream.

1 2 3 4 5 6 7

20. I set my goals higher than I can reach.

1 2 3 4 5 6 7

21. I bite off more than I can chew.

1 2 3 4 5 6 7

22. I am an eternal optimist.

1 2 3 4 5 6 7

23. I don't like to take chances.

1 2 3 4 5 6 7

24. I think something through thoroughly before I act on it.

1 2 3 4 5 6 7

25. After failing at an important task I feel that my life is not worth living.

1 2 3 4 5 6 7

26. I feel I am always rushing.

1 2 3 4 5 6 7

27. I never give up.

1 2 3 4 5 6 7

28. I must do well.

1 2 3 4 5 6 7

29. I push myself to the limit.

1 2 3 4 5 6 7

30. My commitments leave me little time to relax.

1 2 3 4 5 6 7

31. I get high from work.
    1 2 3 4 5 6 7
32. I play by the rules.
    1 2 3 4 5 6 7
33. I carefully consider every possibility before making a
    move.
    1 2 3 4 5 6 7
34. There is virtually nothing I can't do.
    1 2 3 4 5 6 7
35. I tend to move on to the next thing before I finish what I
    am doing.
    1 2 3 4 5 6 7

Scoring Your Test

To score the Performance Zone Profile, you'll need a piece
of paper. Set up six columns: Panic, Drone, C, CM, CF, CT.
These last three represent the Type C characteristics: commitment (CM), confidence (CF) and control (CT).

Now compare your answers from the test with those on
the score sheet, which indicate the point value and performance zone for each possible answer (i.e., a score of 2C = 2
points in the C column). If your score on a particular question falls in the Panic (P) or Drone (D) category, simply add
the point score to that column.

If you score in the C Zone, give yourself the indicated
number of points in the C column. Additionally, when you
score a C, look at column no. 8 on the score sheet to determine the Type C characteristic being tested by that question. (Some questions have only one characteristic, others
two.) Then enter the number of C points you received for
that answer into appropriate Type C characteristic column.
You get CM, CF or CT points only when you have a C score.

For example, let's score question no. 1. If your answer was
a 3, give yourself 1 point in the Drone column. If, on the

other hand, your answer was a 5, give yourself 2 points in the C column and 2 points in both the CF and CT columns.

Interpreting Your Score

Compare your total scores in the first three columns: Panic, Drone and C. Your score will be highest in the zone you occupy the most often. This will give you an indication of how you tend to stray from your C Zone. A Type C generally scores twice as many C points as Drone and Panic points combined.

The CM, CF and CT columns will indicate which Type C characteristics are well developed and which need work. If your strength, in terms of these characteristics, far outweighs your weak points, you may be relying too much on that characteristic and too little on the others. A perfect Type C would score 30 points in each category. But then who's perfect?

Results

The results of the test tell you how you saw yourself at the time you took it. Use this as a general guide to set your priorities for improvement. As you practice the techniques discussed in this book your score will change. Taking the test every few months is a good way to review your development as a C.

Performance Zone Profile

Score Sheet

	1	2	3	4	5	6	7	8
1.	2D	2D	1D	2C	2C	1P	3P	CF/CT
2.	2D	1D	1C	2C	1P	2P	3P	CM/CT
3.	2D	2D	1D	2C	2C	1P	3P	CF
4.	3D	2D	1D	—	2C	1P	3P	CM
5.	2P	2C	2C	1D	2D	3D	3D	CF/CT
6.	3D	3D	2D	1D	2C	1C	2P	CM
7.	3D	2D	1D	1C	2C	1P	2P	CM
8.	3D	3D	2D	1D	2C	2C	2P	CF/CT
9.	—	2C	1C	—	—	—	—	CF
10.	2P	1P	2C	1C	1D	2D	3D	CF
11.	3D	2D	1D	1C	2C	1P	3P	CM
12.	3P	2P	1P	2C	1C	—	1D	CT
13.	2P	1C	2C	—	1D	2D	3D	CF/CT
14.	—	—	1C	2C	—	—	—	CF
15.	3D	3D	2D	1D	2C	1C	2P	CM
16.	3P	1P	2C	—	1D	2D	3D	CF/CT
17.	1D	2C	1C	1P	2P	3P	3P	CT/CM
18.	3D	2D	1D	—	2C	1P	2P	CM
19.	2D	2D	2D	1D	1C	2C	1P	CM
20.	3D	2D	1D	—	2C	1P	3P	CM
21.	3D	2D	1D	1C	2C	1P	3P	CM
22.	3D	2D	1D	1C	2C	1C	2P	CF
23.	2P	2C	2C	1D	2D	3D	3D	CF/CT
24.	3P	3P	2P	1P	2C	—	1D	CT
25.	1C	2C	1C	—	—	—	—	CF
26.	2D	1D	1C	2C	1P	2P	3P	CT
27.	3D	2D	1D	1C	2C	1P	3P	CM
28.	—	—	1C	2C	—	—	—	CF
29.	3D	3D	2D	1D	2C	1P	3P	CM

	1	2	3	4	5	6	7	8
30.	3D	2D	1D	1C	2C	1P	3P	CM/CT
31.	3D	3D	2D	1D	—	2C	2C	CM
32.	2P	1C	2C	—	1D	2D	3D	CF/CT
33.	3P	2P	1P	1C	2C	1D	2D	CT
34.	3D	3D	2D	1D	2C	2C	2P	CF
35.	—	1C	2C	—	—	—	—	CT

CHAPTER FOUR

Obstacles to C Zone Performance: The Vicious Cycle

Riding the Roller Coaster

What stops us from playing in the C Zone all the time? Why does our performance seem to peak and plummet with such maddening unpredictability? Why, at certain times, are we able to meet deadlines with ease, surpass quotas and transform potential problems into great opportunities, while at other times we choke in meetings, find it impossible to get overdue reports finished or feel that sales are harder to come by than snow in the Sahara? You experienced Type C confidence, commitment and control only yesterday. Where did it go? How did you go from the C Zone to the Panic Zone or the Drone Zone so quickly?

Performance Triggers

One of the first things we ask the participants in a seminar to do is to list the types of situations they believe cause them to end up in the Panic Zone or the Drone Zone. The following is a sampling of their responses:

deadlines	speaking in front of large groups
quotas	meetings with senior personnel
changes	new information
budget cuts and reviews	new clients
tight economy	money
competition	Monday morning
new boss	machines breaking down
problems at home	shortage of staff
traffic jams	parking
phones ringing	asking for a raise

This list is based on the assumption that a *situation* causes you to end up in the Panic Zone or the Drone Zone. Take, for example, one situation that seems high on most people's list: talking in front of groups. Has this situation ever not been a problem? Haven't you ever spoken up at a staff meeting or given a good talk?

"Sure," said William T., the program director of a resort conference center, who gives the introductory talk to business groups that come to the facility. "Sometimes I'm relaxed and confident. I tell jokes, and get to know the people in the group. When I'm like that the talk goes great and it's fun, and I make everybody feel at home. Unfortunately that's not usually the case. Often when I get up there to speak I have this little voice in my head that says, 'They didn't come here to listen to you give your spiel. They're not interested in when the pool and tennis courts are open and when meals are served.' When I'm feeling that way I bomb. I try too hard to be funny and I'm flat."

When William thinks the audience is not interested, he becomes nervous and performs poorly. When he doesn't feel that way, he does fine and even has fun. Obviously it's not the talks that take William out of the C Zone. It's his attitude about them.

We recently conducted a program for sales people in a management training business which was being hit hard by the tight economy. It is informative to see how two of these salespeople responded to these tough times.

Louis A. was in the biggest slump of his career. "Everybody's cut their budget for training and a lot of the programs I sold are being canceled. There's just no money around. The way I'm being avoided, I feel like I am peddling a communicable disease. It's gotten to the point that I'm not even making calls. What's the use?"

Charlene M., on the other hand, had gone 25 percent over quota for the previous quarter. "I know the economy is tight and budgets for our programs are being cut. But some people are still buying. I've just got to work harder to find them. Actually the economy has helped me in one way. There's less competition because a lot of companies in the field have laid people off. So when I do find someone who is interested I usually get the order. I've actually opened quite a few new accounts."

Same circumstance, opposite responses. The economy didn't cause Louis to do poorly and Charlene to do well. Attitude did. Louis's defeatist attitude caused him to nosedive into the Drone Zone. Charlene's optimism and confidence about the same situation kept her in the C Zone. She saw the poor economy as a challenge. Situations and tasks are neutral. It is the individual's attitude toward them that determines the zone he will play in and how effective he will be.

Type C performers don't allow circumstances to dictate their performance. They realize that situations do have an effect, but that ultimately it is their attitude about them which makes the difference. "Sure, we have a bad economy and interest rates are high—that's the environment we are in," says Charles A. Lynch, the chief executive officer of SAGA Corporation. "But now's the time to be stronger, to take advantage of the situation. Now's the time to get a jump on the competition by being first and fastest out of the box."

Underscoring this relationship of attitude to performance, Billie Jean King says, "If you believe you will fail, you will find some way to fail."[1] Coming at it from the opposite end, Tom Landry, coach of the Dallas Cowboys, the winningest team in the National Football League for the past ten years, says, "However you think determines how you play."[2]

You See What You Believe

Many people believe that their attitude is caused by what they see; that your fear, as you stand on top of a ski slope, is a result of seeing how steep it is; that your anxiety, as you stand up to speak in a meeting, is caused by seeing the size of the group. But that's usually not true.

Perhaps you had no feelings about skiing the slope or talking to the group before you encountered them, but it's much more likely that you were thinking about taking that steep run while you were riding up the ski lift. It was then, before you actually even saw the slope, that you started to feel anxious and your heart began to beat faster. By the time you got to the top of the run you were already scared. Similarly, you probably started feeling anxious when you first knew you were going to speak in that meeting.

What you see is not what is actually before your eyes but what's *projected* by your attitude. Projecting your attitude onto a situation is like putting a colored filter over the lens of your camera. Everything you see is colored by that filter. Your attitude colors your perception of a situation just as the filter does. Doubts or fears cause you to see the situation through a screen; everything becomes clouded by your apprehension and appears more threatening than it is. Ski slopes look frighteningly steep and the people to whom you are speaking look unreceptive and even hostile.

Baseball player Mike Schmidt, twice voted the Most Valuable Player in the National League, says that when you are in a slump and worried about it, all you see are obstacles on the field that will prevent your ball from dropping in for a hit. Even the second-base umpire appears to be wearing a glove at these times.[3]

Your attitude not only colors your perception of a situation; it actually seeks out that which will reinforce it.

Ann G., a department store buyer, talks of this phenomenon. "The day before a big sale I'm always concerned with making sure that all the markdowns are correct and that all the specials are on the floor. I'm panicked that I'll never finish on time and my department will be the only one that isn't ready.

"At these times, I have an uncanny ability to notice only the salespeople who aren't actively working on the sale preparation. It seems to me that everyone is either on a coffee break, standing around talking or spending too much time with a customer who isn't buying.

"This gets me even more anxious and short-tempered. By this point, I have completely lost track of all that's been done and overlook all the people who are working hard on the preparation."

By paying attention only to those people who confirm and reinforce her fear, Ann's anxiety takes her into her Panic Zone.

The Vicious Cycle

A negative attitude not only colors your immediate perception and causes you to seek out confirmation; it also has an insidious effect on your behavior. It winds into other areas of your life, becoming a vicious cycle that affects everything you do and keeps you out of your C Zone.

The following incident illustrates this vicious cycle effect. Susan E. was a single mother of two children in her early thirties. After her children were out of diapers she went to graduate school for her M.B.A. When she earned her degree, the company she worked for as a student intern hired her as an assistant product manager. Within three years she was the director of new product development and at the time we met her she had been responsible for two very successful product introductions. Although she was highly regarded in the company and liked her work, Susan felt underpaid and was having difficulty making ends meet. When the company announced a wage freeze she decided to look for a higher-paying job.

Her first interview was for a product management job in the same field, one for which she knew she was extremely well qualified. Although her recommendations and her track record were very good, Susan was worried. Her attitude didn't reflect her experience. She felt that she didn't come across well in interviews. She worried that her M.B.A., a requirement for this job, wasn't from a name school.

Susan described how she felt as she sat waiting in the reception room to be interviewed. "My heart was pounding, my palms were sweating. I felt like I was fourteen and about to go on my first date. I couldn't concentrate on the magazine I was reading. A man and a woman were also waiting to be interviewed. I couldn't take my eyes off them. They both looked relaxed and sure of themselves and seemed so professional, which made me even more nervous. Suddenly I was only aware of how frumpy I looked. My hair wasn't right that day. My attaché case looked like it came from a discount store. I noticed a spot on my suit."

When her name was called, Susan said, her knees "felt like water." The interviewer appeared to frown when she came into his office. She smiled feebly as she sat down and right away began to talk too fast and say too much. "When he asked me questions my mind seemed like a jumble of words. There was so much that I wanted to tell him about what I was doing. But it kept coming out wrong. Then I'd have to correct myself. When he looked at the clock on his desk my heart sank. I was sure he was in a hurry and I wanted to make certain I told him everything, so I continued to rush through more of my qualifications."

Afterward Susan realized that she had neglected to mention several accomplishments that were relevant to the job. She felt that she had done terribly in the interview and was depressed as she headed back to her office. The rejection letter she received three days later confirmed her original belief that she wasn't good at interviewing.

The diagram below illustrates that how you perceive a situation and how well you perform is a result of your attitude. Susan's belief that she wouldn't do well made her tense and nervous before she even got to the interview. Her projection of her fear and lack of confidence onto the situation made the interview seem very threatening. It also made the other people waiting in the reception area appear more confident and much more professional than she. This made her even more tense and resulted in a poor performance.

Susan's lack of confidence in this situation caused her to

lose control of herself and perform poorly. Her Panic Zone performance reinforced her lack of confidence about interviewing, which would make it that much harder for her to perform in her C Zone in subsequent interviews.

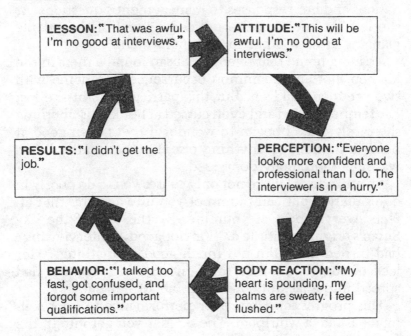

LESSON: "That was awful. I'm no good at interviews."

ATTITUDE: "This will be awful. I'm no good at interviews."

RESULTS: "I didn't get the job."

PERCEPTION: "Everyone looks more confident and professional than I do. The interviewer is in a hurry."

BEHAVIOR: "I talked too fast, got confused, and forgot some important qualifications."

BODY REACTION: "My heart is pounding, my palms are sweaty. I feel flushed."

Poor Performance to Low Self-Esteem: The Making of a Slump

Once you are out of your C Zone, a vicious cycle gets established and begins to affect everything you do. When Susan got back to her office after the interview she was in a foul mood and lost her temper at her secretary over a small error. In a brainstorming meeting for new products, at which she usually performed as a Type C, providing energy and creative spark, Susan was very tentative and unfocused. "I couldn't get my mind off that damn interview."

Later that day, at a monthly progress review with senior management, she was halfhearted in her recommendations and her responses to management's questions. As she left the meeting she noticed several of the people glancing at each other in disappointment.

Arriving home that evening, Susan found a mess in the kitchen, not an uncommon occurrence in a home with two pre-teen children. But this particular night she lost her temper, yelled and even cursed at her kids, something she rarely did. "I began to wonder if I was even good at being a mother, or anything else, for that matter." She was now thoroughly depressed.

An attitude of failure not only causes you to do poorly in one situation but can plummet you into a slump that affects every aspect of your life. By the end of the day Susan's original attitude of "I'm not good at interviewing" had turned into "I'm not much good at anything." Her lack of confidence regarding one specific situation had spread into a lack of confidence about herself.

This progression from poor performance to poor self-image is like a whirlpool. The deeper you get into it, the faster it spins, pulling you down and making it more difficult to get out. Your C Zone, from the bottom of the whirlpool, seems totally out of reach.

The whirlpool effect looks like this:

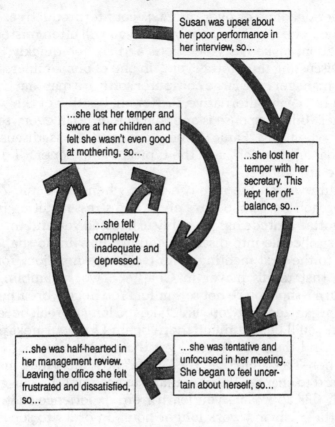

"I Gotta": A Panic Zone Vicious Cycle

The Panic Zone vicious cycle most prevalent in today's high-pressure work world starts with a "Gotta" attitude: "I gotta make this deadline!" "I gotta make this sale!" "I gotta finish this report!" "I gotta be the best!"

The "gotta" attitude will sometimes provide a quick boost of energy. But the stress and tension that result from trying to do more in less time, so that you can come in under deadline or over quota, is counterproductive. In a Panic Zone rush to get a job done you will often misread a situation, make hasty decisions and act too quickly.

Discussing the "gotta cycle" in one of our seminars, Bill J., a manager for a large computer software manufacturer, said he saw no alternative. "After all, I gotta get the work done!" Bill's response is one that comes up in every seminar when this Panic Zone vicious cycle is discussed. "What am I to do?" asks the typical Panic Zoner. "I don't have any choice!"

But even on the rare occasions when this Panic Zone approach works, the extra effort and stress resulting from a "gotta" attitude has probably exhausted you and thrown your schedule into disarray. You are now in no shape to get to the next meeting or to tackle the next job. You're like that tennis player in Chapter Two, scrambling to return a shot you're not set up for. You need a breather to get organized. But you can't take too long a break because then you'll be that much more behind for your next project. And then you "gotta" get that one done too.

There's a Catch-22 in the "gotta" attitude which makes it hard to change. If you manage to accomplish your goals with this approach, you learn from experience that you "gotta" rush and work longer hours in order to succeed. On the other hand, if you don't succeed with this approach, you learn that you've "gotta" try even harder next time. Either way, the vicious cycle is reinforced and you remain in the Panic Zone. Eventually the "gotta" gets you!

The Drone Zone Vicious Cycle: "I Can't"

Both Panic Zoners and Drone Zoners lack confidence but their response to pressure is different. The Panic Zoner thinks "I gotta." The Drone Zoner's attitude under pressure is "I can't" and he takes few risks. When he does act, he does so halfheartedly, expecting and ensuring poor performance. "I was right," he thinks, "it was too difficult." His lack of confidence has been reinforced.

It is not the difficulty of the task that brings about the Drone Zoner's poor performance. It is his "I can't" attitude, which, reinforced by failure, will continue to prevent him from taking effective action.

Vicious Cycle

Think of a situation in which you typically perform poorly and answer the following questions at the appropriate places on the diagram.

1. Situation . . .
2. Attitude—when confronted with this situation.
3. Perception—how the situation appears to me; how I perceive it.
4. Body—my physical response to the situation; what I feel.
5. Behavior—how I perform in this situation; what I do.
6. Results—how things turn out; how I do.
7. Lesson—what I learn from this situation.

LESSON: _____   ATTITUDE: _____

RESULTS: _____   PERCEPTION: _____

BEHAVIOR: _____   BODY REACTION: _____

The Vital Cycle: Type C Behavior

In one of my seminars I asked the members of a top college basketball team to imagine they were on the foul line in the last seconds of a championship game; their team was down by one point. If they made both points they would win. If not . . .

"What is going on in your mind as you stand there waiting to shoot?" I asked.

"I'm thinking about what would happen if I missed."

"I've got to get it in."

"I'll never be able to look my friends in the eye if I miss."

"A blur."

I was about to go into an explanation of the vicious cycle when a big forward, whom I later found out was an honorable-mention All-American, said, "Hey, I wouldn't be thinking about any of those things. That just messes me up. I love those tight spots. They're my chance to get some good ink, to be a hero. Hell, I've made ninety-five out of a hundred foul shots in practice. Sinking that shot is a snap! I concentrate on the back of the rim, just like I do in practice. Just me and the basket. I don't even hear the crowd. The basket even begins to look bigger." Then he took a deep breath, exhaled slowly, faked a shot and laughed. "Right in."

This athlete's Type C attitude, based on his experience, helped him perceive the situation optimistically, which enabled him to concentrate more intensely and perform at his best. He created a vital cycle for himself.

A Type C attitude initiates a vital cycle in which one Type C episode follows another.

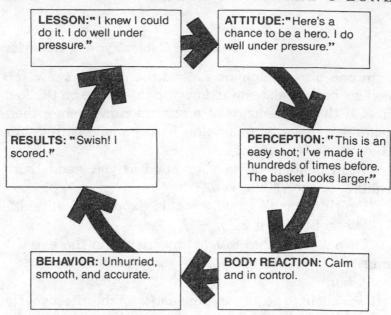

The Ripple Effect: One Vital Cycle Leads to Another

Vital cycles constantly expand like ripples in a lake into which a stone has been thrown. One Type C episode leads to another . . . and another . . .

Imagine the effect on the rest of Susan's day and evening if she had had a Type C attitude about herself in that interview, the way she normally had in her job. It would have carried over into her brainstorming session, into the meeting with senior management and with her children at home.

Vital Cycle

Think of a situation where you perform in your C Zone. Fill out the questions below in the appropriate places on the diagram.

1. Situation . . .
2. Attitude—when confronted with this situation.
3. Perception—how the situation appears to me; how I perceive it.
4. Body—my physical response to the situation; what I feel.
5. Behavior—how I perform in this situation; what I do.
6. Results—how things turn out; how I do.
7. Lesson—what I learn from this situation.

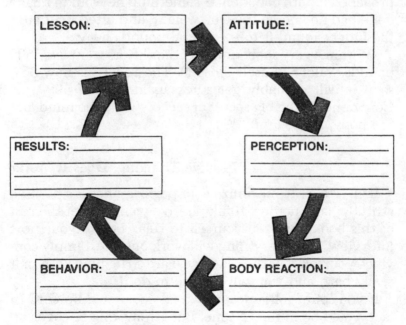

A Record-Breaking Attitude

Discussing the effect of a confident attitude on performance, Arnold Schwarzenegger, five-time winner of the Mr. Universe contest, referred to the 500-pound barrier in the clean-and-jerk event in weight lifting, which was similar in its formidability to the old four-minute mile. "No one could lift it," Schwarzenegger tells it, "and because the media made such a big deal out of this 500-pound barrier, all the lifters were greatly intimidated. They would stand in front of the bar thinking, 'How can I lift 500? No one has ever done it before.' Therefore nobody did it.

"Finally Valery Alexis, the world-record holder at 499, came to lift. He was told the bar was at 499 and approached it with confidence, something he wouldn't have done had he known the true weight, and lifted it." Later, the judges found it to be several pounds heavier.

"Within a very short time six other lifters went over 500 pounds. Valery himself did 520. The record is now 564, soon it will probably get stuck again around 599. . . . Confidence is the big secret of success . . . the mind, not the body, is the limit."[4]

Positive Thinking: Does It Work?

If all it takes to maximize your performance is a positive attitude, why not just think positively and forget the rest of this book? Just tell yourself to relax before your next interview, and everything will work out fine. Simply convince yourself that the report you are struggling with isn't really hard and you will be able to do it.

If you *could* follow your own advice, you'd be O.K. In fact, you'd be in the C Zone. But attempting to cover up

fear or lack of confidence by talking yourself into a positive attitude is like trying to smother a fire with a card-
board box. Your fear, like the fire, may momentarily sub-
side, but then it flares up even higher. In the same way,
your tension increases the more you tell yourself when
under pressure: "Relax, dammit!"

Larry Holmes, the current heavyweight champion of
the world, said, "If my mind can conceive it and my heart
can believe it, I will achieve it."[5] Merely telling yourself to
relax in tight situations is as futile as trying to get your
mind to conceive something your heart doesn't believe.
In fact, it's the same thing.

Positive thinking doesn't work to keep you in your C
Zone as easily as some would have us believe. Attitude,
which is what determines performance, involves much
more than conscious thoughts. Attitude is influenced by
feelings, instincts, mental pictures and physical conditions. Conscious thoughts, the only ingredient in positive
thinking, are just a small part of attitude. In fact, they are
more the result of your attitude than the cause. Trying to
change a negative attitude with positive thinking is therefore usually futile and frustrating.

Transforming Vicious Cycles to Vital Cycles

Vicious cycles can be broken and vital ones begun by
increasing your confidence, commitment or control. The
techniques for developing your Type C characteristics are
simple, easy to implement, and most important, they
work. You can use them as many peak performers do
when *preparing* for an important event. You can also use
these techniques *during* pressure situations in order to
decrease stress, concentrate better, express yourself more
clearly and be calm and sure under fire.

Each of the techniques discussed in the next chapters

will help you develop a specific Type C characteristic. Just as one vital cycle leads to another, increasing your strength in one Type C characteristic strengthens the others as well. Increasing your confidence will therefore lead to increased self-control and a deeper commitment and vice versa. You can't lose. Any of the techniques described in the following chapters will lead you into your C Zone.

CHAPTER FIVE

Increasing Commitment: Doing What You Love

Commitment is the characteristic most frequently mentioned as being critical for operating in the C Zone. "People lacking in other areas have made it to the top, but nobody I know has become successful without having a strong commitment," Gary Shansby, the chief executive officer of the Shaklee Corporation, told us.

Luckily for the great majority of us who aren't naturally gifted, a strong commitment is more valuable than natural talent. Former Women's PGA rookie of the year Jan Stephenson, who is now one of the leading money winners in women's golf, is not a great natural athlete. "Not even close, according to her coach, other golfers and even in her own estimation . . . Yet she has one of the most consistent drives in the game, a marvelous wedge shot . . . a great putter."[1]

Commitment is the secret of Stephenson's success. She practices more than other golfers. "I'd rather practice

than play socially," Stephenson says. "If friends . . .
want me to join them I won't do it. I'd much rather hit
balls . . ."[2]

"Many top executives don't have a lot more ability than
the next guy," says Tom Simpson. "Their ticket to the top
is an incredibly strong commitment. I have also seen people who by virtue of brains alone should have made it to
the top. Yet because they didn't have the desire and commitment they never made it."

Desire: The Spark of Commitment

"Desire is the starting point of all achievement," wrote
Napoleon Hill, ". . . not a hope, not a wish, but a keen
pulsating desire which transcends everything."[3] The
Type C's commitment is sparked by a desire which impels
them to pursue that which they love. "The biggest predic-
tor of success . . . is a strong preference for the work,"
says peak-performance researcher Dr. Charles Garfield.
"It's even more important than aptitude for the job itself."[4]

"I love what I do and couldn't imagine doing anything
else." This statement by Walter Freese, senior vice-president and chief financial officer of Doubleday, was typical
of the Type C's attitude toward his work.

Tony Tiano, the president of San Francisco's public television station KQED, told us that he never works. "What I
mean is that I enjoy it so much it doesn't ever seem to be
work."

Howard Head, who revolutionized skiing when he in-
vented the first metal ski, talked the same way about his
career. "I just love design. If it weren't fun I wouldn't do
it."[5]

"The thing I love best in the world is playing and winning," says Jimmy the Greek, the well-known oddsmaker
and TV personality. "Second best is playing and losing."

If you recall your own Type C episodes, you were, in those moments, loving what you were doing and doing what you loved. *Type C commitment is essentially a commitment to yourself.* It is knowing what you want, honoring your innermost desires and translating them into action.

Are You Doing What You Want?

Judd B. was a sales representative for several major office supply manufacturers. For the past six years he had done well financially. But recently he had been in a slump. "I can't pinpoint the problem," he told us. "But I don't feel as motivated as I used to. A couple of months ago I set some goals as a way of getting myself going. I was sure I would accomplish them but I haven't even gotten close. I don't understand it," he said, "the plan was great. I just couldn't get myself to stick to it."

We asked him to imagine himself achieving the objectives he had set. He saw himself calling on new clients, making presentations, closing sales, being successful and even hiring a few salesmen to expand his agency.

But something was wrong. Although he was saying all the "right" things, there was no enthusiasm in his voice. He didn't seem excited about the prospects he was describing. He sounded as if he was in the Drone Zone, going through the motions.

When we asked him about his lack of enthusiasm, he said, "You know, as I watched myself accomplishing all my goals I had a disturbing thought. 'Hell, I'm doing the same thing I'm doing now, only working a little harder.' I realized that I wasn't turned on or excited by what I was doing. Sure, I was making more money, but that didn't cut it. It didn't make what I was doing any more satisfying or fulfilling. I was still doing the same thing for eight to ten hours a day and not enjoying it. I realized I was working for the money but that it no longer energized or motivated me."

Judd had diagnosed his lack of motivation as simply a lack of goals. He had then set clearly defined objectives and strategies as a means of remedying his situation, a common approach to this type of problem. But his plan didn't work. Something basic was missing. The problem was that deep down Judd didn't *like* what he was doing. He was, as many in similar positions are, not committed to the goals he had set, which would make them very difficult to achieve.

Setting goals to create motivation is putting the cart before the horse. Desire determines direction, not the other way around. When goals are set without commitment we inevitably hit a crisis, as Judd did. We discover that what we are doing is not meaningful and we aren't motivated to accomplish our goals.

Commitment Check

An awareness of those things that you want to do and a sensitivity to those that you don't are a prerequisite for developing commitment.

The things we do all day are in fact the activities to which we have committed our time and energy.

Make a list of the things you do each day at work and home; include all your significant activities. Then mark each activity on a scale of 1–10, with the high end of the scale being reflective of a commitment to yourself and the things you want and enjoy doing.

Prepare your list thoroughly. Be specific.

Look over your list. Note how you are spending your time. Are you doing what you want to be doing?

See if any of the activities given low scores are actually a necessary, but unenjoyable, part of a larger activity from which satisfaction is derived—i.e., packing for a trip, preparing budget plans for a new product, making out your expense account, preparing recommendations, answering phone calls.

The activities which are on the low end of your scale, can be an important source of information to you. Dissatisfaction can lead to finding creative ways of bringing your current work more in line with what you want. It can also lead you to begin to pursue other work that may be to your liking and to which you can make a deeper commitment.

Doing What Comes Naturally

Commitment can't be forced. No motivational gimmicks, inspirational speeches or goal-setting sessions can make up for your Type C natural energy and motivation that come from doing what you enjoy and want to do.

People whose goals aren't based on a strong commitment end up in the Panic Zone or the Drone Zone. Panic Zoners rev up and try too hard to make up for their lack of natural commitment. Drone Zoners fall into a state of apathy, uninspired and not really caring whether or not they accomplish their goals.

Harmony between what you do and what you want to do is imperative for commitment and C Zone performance. The ambivalence that occurs from lack of commitment impairs performance. Energy and attention are split. It's like being pulled in two directions.

When Judd did the commitment check it turned out he had a passion for writing ads. He spent his spare time creating commercials for some of his clients' products. He even took a course in copywriting, "just for the fun of it." Instead of preparing his calls for the next day he had been attending a copywriting class and working on experimental ad campaigns.

Rather than starting with external goals and trying to get motivated to achieve them, Type C's start from the inside. They commit to what they really like and want to do and *then* develop goals and strategies to achieve them. When you are doing what you want, you give 100 percent attention, energy and effort. Type C's know that their level of commitment determines their level of performance.

Commitment Leads to High Performance

Loving what you are doing and C Zone performance are directly related. "Skiing has to be enjoyable or you can't be successful," says Bill Koch, Olympic silver medalist in cross-country skiing.[6] And Debbie Armstrong, gold medalist in the giant slalom in the 1984 Winter Olympics, psyched herself up in the starting gate by chanting, "Have fun! Have fun!"[7]

When you enjoy what you are doing commitment is automatic and natural. If you love the game no one has to make you go out and play tennis. You will look for excuses. You'll read tennis magazines, wander around tennis stores checking out the latest equipment, talk to other tennis buffs about places to play, strategies and strokes. You might even go to a tennis ranch for a vacation. Loving the game inspires a full commitment which helps you to improve dramatically and perform at your peak more consistently.

Working at something that turns you on inspires the same natural commitment, resulting in total involvement and high performance.

As a young man, Jack O'Neil loved the water. He surfed, scuba-dived, fished and always managed to work in or around water. O'Neil was bothered that the wet suits he and other surfers were using leaked and didn't keep out the cold very well. His desire to spend more time in the water heightened his commitment to finding some material that would be leakproof and warm. He began experimenting. Today he owns a multimillion-dollar business that is the largest manufacturer of wet suits in the world.

Commitment Makes Things Seem Easier

The more committed you are to something, the less difficult it appears to be. Anything seems possible when you really want it. Nothing seems too much trouble or too difficult. Obstacles are hurdles to be overcome. Setbacks are seen as opportunities to learn and lead to continued progress.

On the other hand, when commitment is low everything seems overwhelming. The smallest obstacles appear insurmountable. Everything becomes too much trouble, too difficult. Energy and enthusiasm are low. It feels as if you have to push through a wall of resistance to accomplish anything.

The higher the commitment, the more doable a task appears. Confidence increases. Therefore, when two people, one a committed Type C, the other not, look at the same task, they perceive it differently. The Type C sees opportunities, the other obstacles. The committed C looks at the positive aspects and sees what can be done. The uncommitted person only sees what can't be done and is easily discouraged.

Daydreaming: Finding Out What You Really Want

To find out what they really want, Type C's dream. Dreams reflect desires. They are a first step to discovering what you are naturally committed to. A visualization technique that we call daydreaming can help to transform your unconscious desires into conscious commitments. Daydreaming can give you a picture from which the nucleus of a direction and clearly defined goals can be developed.

Daydreaming

To get the most out of your daydream, make sure you won't be interrupted.

RELAX
(Take three or four deep breaths.)

Imagine yourself five years from now doing exactly what you want. Let your imagination soar. Don't censor or edit out anything even if it seems irrational, impossible or unrealistic. Dreams often seem unreal. But in the unreality is a symbolic representation of what you really want. Let your inner camera roll. Allow yourself to be surprised.

See where you are; what you are doing; who you are with; how you look; how it feels, everything . . . Fill in all the details. Watch it as you would a movie. Let the picture come to you rather than consciously trying to create it. Be receptive to your imagination. Let your right brain, the part that controls intuition and creativity, take over.

Following your visualization, while it is still fresh in mind, think of a few words that reflect the quality or essence of your imagery. These "seed" words (see below) are a first step toward transforming your dreams into reality. They will serve as guidelines to keep you inspired and headed in the right direction.

Repeat the exercise often. The more you allow yourself to daydream, the clearer and more detailed these dreams become. And you'll get additional insights into and information about what you really want.

Examples of Seed Words

independent	daring	creating
loving	relaxing	writing
productive	performing	teaching
visible	powerful	rich
committed	challenging	fun
selling	excited	challenging
peaceful	contributing	courageous
playing	directing	mastering

Carole's Dream

After six years of pioneering work in mediation, Carole D., a family lawyer, had a successful practice, a good reputation in the field, and was frequently called upon to speak at professional conferences. But she no longer felt as motivated as she once was and had begun to feel restless. She wanted to do something else but didn't know what.

In her daydream, "I saw myself as tricoastal," she said, "with places in New York and California and a condo in Spain. I was working hard. I was still teaching mediation but doing it through writing books and articles and giving talks and training seminars in the States and Europe. I felt as invigorated as I did when I first started doing this work. But I also saw myself taking walks on the beach, having coffee in a bistro . . ."

She stopped in the middle of that thought and said, "Oh, it all sounds wonderful but it's a fantasy. I can't make that happen. It's unrealistic and I'm just setting myself up for disappointment."

After being told that it didn't have to make sense, that it was just a picture that would help shape her goals, she continued. "Well, I see myself giving talks around the country to college and professional groups, and writing a lot. But also having a lot of time to myself to do what I want. I want to read, write letters to old friends and just plain have some fun. I also see myself traveling to places I always wanted to go, like Russia, China, Bali."

The seed words she chose for her daydream were "independent," "creative," "relaxed" and "productive."

Carole's tricoastal dream was a broad general picture that provided her with direction and inspired commitment. Using her seed words, she shaped this dream into a tangible long-term goal that involved making speeches, training professionals, writing books and articles and also relaxing and traveling a lot.

She then began to develop specific short-term goals that would help her realize her dream. After six months Carole had reached her first goal, which was to be giving a minimum of one speech or training program a month. She had also begun writing an article for a law journal.

After two years she had taken on a partner to handle her private practice. She was giving three to four speeches a month and had four articles published. She doesn't have her condo in Spain, but she does travel frequently between New York and California and takes a lot of walks on the beach.

Many daydreams are less specific in terms of content than Carole's. In these cases the imagery doesn't give a clear picture of what to do next, but the seed words, which describe the essence of the "dream," provide guidelines for the direction to take.

The seed words that Arthur D., a successful but burned-out independent documentary-film producer came up with as a result of his daydream were: relationships, communication, fun. "That's it," he said, "I really don't want to get out of film making. I think what I need is to begin working more with other people. Working by myself can get very lonely. Having some people to collaborate with would be much more fun and probably more mentally stimulating as well."

Seed words indicate qualities that often need further development or are missing from your current career or life-style. Many people, like Arthur D., learn from their daydreams, and resulting seed words, that it is not their work but the way they are doing it that is the source of their dissatisfaction.

Goal Setting: Turning Dreams to Reality

Type C's make their dreams come true. They translate inner desires to the outer world. Using their daydreams and seed words as guidelines, they develop goals and action plans for accomplishing them.

Describing this process of moving from a dream to a reality, from a general direction to a specific goal, Arch McGill, former president of AT&T's Advance Information Systems division, says, "I operate out of a vision . . . that I have in my mind's eye. My visions start out intuitively. I add fiber and substance as I get closer."

Type C's set goals to channel the energy sparked by their desire. With a clear set of commitment-based goals, the Type C uses time and energy more efficiently. Priorities are more obvious. Choices are clearer.

Bifocal Vision: Present and Future Focus

There is a time for goals and dreams, and there is a time for performance. Jan Stephenson blew her last shot in a big tournament because she was thinking too much about winning. "It [making that shot] would have boosted me to no. 2 on the winners list. I would have passed Nancy [Lopez] and I was setting up my shot thinking of that instead of what I was doing."[8] The more your attention is focused on the future, your goal, the less your attention is on the present, on what you are doing now. The chance for error is increased.

This tendency to focus exclusively on the future—to pay attention only to where you are going and not to where you are—is typical of the Panic Zoner. This type is always trying to be ten steps ahead of where he is. In his rush to reach the goal, the Panic Zoner takes on too much, tries to do it too quickly and gets in over his head. Sacrificing quality, he never takes time to master skills, attend to details, think creatively, plan effectively or analyze feedback.

On the other hand, Drone Zoners lose sight of their dreams and lose motivation and direction. They get caught up in the morass of what seem to be meaningless everyday tasks. Forgetting where they are going and why they want to get there, Drones feel like they are going nowhere and doing nothing.

Type C's use bifocal vision. They shuttle their attention back and forth between the present and the future. Focus on goals maintains vision, direction and motivation. Focus on the present situation maximizes performance by increasing control and concentration.

Visualizing your goal daily will put your everyday work into a larger perspective and put you in the C Zone. Reminding yourself of your dreams will give your work more meaning and purpose, keep you inspired and help you make appropriate and wise decisions.

While working toward his Mr. Universe titles Arnold Schwarzenegger would visualize his goal, seeing in his mind the finished product for which he was aiming. "Knowing where you are going," Schwarzenegger says, "makes it so much easier . . . You focus right in . . . on your vision, on your image, and that's why you're there for four hours—to get a step closer."[9]

Visualizing Your Goal

Spend a little time each day visualizing yourself accomplishing your goal. See and feel it in as much detail as possible. Experience the joy that comes with accomplishment.

Type C Commitment

Once you have your goal in mind you need to refocus your attention on what you are doing. If you get bogged down, and begin to feel like chucking it all, take a few minutes to revisualize your goal. Remind yourself what you are there for and where you are going.

Focusing on the future provides energy and direction. Paying attention to the present maximizes performance and progress. The shuttle between your vision and your process will reinforce Type C commitment and maximize Type C behavior. In every case, the possibility for Type C behavior is increased when you are doing what you love and love what you are doing.

Type C commitment, the commitment to one's dreams and visions, will provide you with the drive and energy to overcome many of the obstacles to C Zone behavior.

CHAPTER SIX

Increasing
C Zone Confidence:
Overcoming Fear

Lack of Confidence

It's no news that confidence is critical for peak performance and success. Confidence is key for starting vital
cycles and operating in your C Zone. But the confidence
that keeps you in your C Zone is not just confidence in
your ability to perform. It is confidence in yourself, an
experience of your own self-worth that radiates out into
everything you do.

C Zone confidence doesn't depend upon your performance; nor does it fluctuate with other people's moods,
how you look or the political climate in your office. It is a
constant positive experience of yourself that is not dependent upon anything external. "I don't believe I am what I
am . . . because of what I do outside but because of what
I am inside," says Yannick Noah, the fourth-ranked tennis
player in the world in 1983.[1]

Confidence in your ability is finite and continually

changing with every situation you are in. Confidence in yourself is constant.

To know that your self-confidence isn't always on the line, to be independent of performance, is very liberating. It frees you to commit yourself more fully, to take more chances, to be more creative and to experience more joy in whatever you do.

The main obstacle to C Zone confidence is fear. Fear blocks your innate Type C self-confidence from being translated into action. Fear drives you out of the C Zone and into either a Panic Zone frenzy or a Drone Zone freeze. The way you handle this threat to your confidence will determine the zone in which you perform.

"You can't be a winner and be afraid to lose," said SAGA Corporation's Charles Lynch. "It's antithetical to success. Fear will prevent you from feeling confident enough to call on those big clients and play in the big leagues."

Fear of Failing

Peter J. is vice-president and creative director for one of the world's largest advertising agencies. His income is well into six figures and he has won many awards for his TV commercials. He has an apartment in the city, a house in the country and two children in college. Everyone who knows Peter says "he has it made." Everyone except Peter himself.

"I originally got into the ad business as a way to make some money while I became a writer. Well, here I am at forty-five and I haven't written a thing. I have an idea for a great screenplay but I never start working on it. I'm afraid it's not going to be good enough, and afraid of what that will say about me. So I continue working on these ads even though my heart's not in it."

Dr. Rachel D. is head nutritionist for a large breakfast

cereal manufacturer. She is well known in her field, and frequently called upon to speak at major conferences, write articles for professional journals and advise on new products. Her phone is always ringing and someone is always popping into her office for advice and help on their projects or personal diets.

Rachel's problem is setting limits. "I make myself endlessly accessible because I'm afraid that any article I say no to writing will have been the one to have made a difference for the company and for my reputation. Every speaking engagement feels like an obligation and that I'm going to offend and alienate people in the industry whose cooperation I need if I don't take it.

"To make matters worse, I'm afraid to even close my office door because word will get out that I've become highfalutin and inaccessible and I'll lose all the friendships I've developed over the years. As a result, I say yes to everything and everyone. I'm constantly in over my head. I don't have time to get my work done; all I do is run around taking care of everybody else."

Fear is the main impediment to the self-confidence needed to perform in the C Zone. Peter's fear of failing to meet an imaginary standard robs him of the confidence needed to challenge himself and take the risk to write his screenplay. Thus he remains in his Drone Zone, frustrated and disappointed despite his many accomplishments, but still unwilling to leave his safe place.

Rachel's fear of failing to make the most of opportunities and to please others causes her to lack the confidence to establish priorities and say no when she needs to. Because she tries to do too much, she feels over her head and out of control and ends up in her Panic Zone.

Losing Is a Part of Winning

James Robinson, America's best 800-meter runner and six-time national champion, began losing races last year. Robinson said, "I'm not afraid of losing; losing is part of being a champion. I feel a champion is one who can lose and then bounce back."[2]

Type C performers may hate to fail, but they aren't *afraid* to. "Losing is a part of winning," Dick Munroe, the chief executive officer of Time Inc., told us. "It's like playing tennis. You're always going to lose a few points, a couple of games and even some sets. If you don't, you're not challenging yourself. If you're afraid of losing you'll hold back. You don't hit winners that way. The same is true in any area of life. If you're afraid to fail, you'll lack the confidence needed to go all out and give it everything you've got. If you are afraid to lose, you'll never win." Sounds like a Catch-22? It is.

Type C performers know that in this rapidly changing time they have to be innovative, to take risks, to confront the many challenges set forth by this new age. They also know that with risk come mistakes and failures. The chief executive officer of the Koppers Company, Fletcher Byrom, has a Ninth Commandment: Make sure you generate a reasonable number of mistakes.[3]

Mistakes or failures aren't obstacles to Type C behavior. The fear of them is.

Fear is Natural

Fear is a normal response to pressure. Even top professionals experience it before performing. Helen Hayes says she goes stone deaf on opening nights. Ann Miller gets dizzy and nauseated, and Estelle Parsons can't shake a deep feeling of lethargy. "The very idea of speaking to a group, much less before a big audience, was enough to make my heart pound and my mouth go dry," said Gloria Steinem.[4]

Many top athletes experience the same type of "stage fright" before a game. Bill Russell, one of the greatest basketball players ever, used to throw up before some games. Olympic gold medalist and world-record holder in the 400-meter hurdles, Edwin Moses, who has not lost in one hundred races, says that each time he races, "it feels like I'm being led to my execution."[5]

"Everyone experiences a certain amount of anxiety," says Coca-Cola president Don Keough. "The adrenaline is flowing; the anxiety builds an inner tension . . . and you can feel your blood pressure bouncing and your heart pounding." But, he adds, "you learn that it can be positive rather than negative."[6]

You can't stop fear from happening. You can learn to handle it. Type C's experience fear but have learned to use the tremendous energy that it generates to break through to higher levels of performance.

Fear Factors

To learn how to increase your C Zone confidence in fearful situations, you must first understand how fear works.

Many years ago I was backpacking with a group of people in the Sierras. In the evening we were told to hang our food high in a tree so that bears wouldn't steal it. Being new to the West, I had never seen a bear outside of a zoo. I had heard horror stories about how big, strong and fast they were, and how they mutilated people in their sleeping bags while foraging for their food. I was afraid that the food the bears would find would be me.

When it came time to go to sleep, I was petrified. I put my sleeping bag down near the fire in the middle of the group. It didn't matter that the ground there was full of rocks. I figured it was the last place the bears would hit. As I lay there with my heart pounding, sleep was impossible. Every sound was a bear. Someone rolling over was a bear moving. The wind blowing through the trees was a bear sneaking up on me. When the moon created shadows through the trees, it was a bear right there next to me.

Usually, the problem isn't ferocious bears. But critical clients or tight deadlines are no different; your mind plays tricks on you when you are afraid. Remote improbabilities seem realistic possibilities. Fear distorts your perception, making situations look more dangerous and difficult than they really are, while your ability to handle them appears diminished. And what might happen IF . . . is too awful to even think about.

The Telescope Effect: Making a Mountain Out of a Molehill

Fear blocks Type C confidence by causing your imagination to run wild. Everything seems more difficult and dangerous than it is. Cus D'Amato, the legendary fight manager, talks about how young fighters entering the ring for the first time usually scare themselves into losing. "The young fighter always perceives his first-time opponent as being bigger, stronger and faster than he is," says D'Amato.[7]

When we are anxious and stressed on the job we distort reality in the same way. Situations seem much more difficult and more important than they really are. You walk into your office worried about meeting a deadline, and the pile of papers on your desk appears mountainous. You feel as if the presentation you have to give, the report you must submit or the sale you have to make involves life-or-death consequences.

At times like this, as in any vicious cycle, we tend to notice only those things that reinforce and increase our fear. A frightened skier only sees huge bumps and ice, and doesn't observe that most of the slope is easy. A fear-filled speaker only notices the person in the audience who is yawning and looking at his watch, and doesn't realize that everyone else is listening intently.

Fear causes you to perceive a situation as if you were alternately looking through each end of a telescope. The difficulty or importance of the task is greatly magnified as you look through one end. Your ability to perform is minimized as you look through the other. These distorted views reinforce your fear, which blocks your Type C confidence and prevents you from operating in the C Zone.

"Or Else": The Doomsday Syndrome

"I was afraid of failure," said baseball player Mike Schmidt. "I'd go up and squeeze the bat and say, 'I've got to get a hit.'"[8] But "Gotta" is really only half a thought. The other half is the "or else"; the consequences you fear if you fail to do what you think you've "gotta."

The consequences Schmidt feared, if he didn't get a hit, were: "50,000 people will boo me" or "I'll lose that contract."[9] The fear that exaggerates the difficulty of a situation also exaggerates the imagined consequences. You act as if any fall on the ski slope will result in a broken leg or the consequences of losing a sale will be losing your job.

Fear magnifies the consequences of failing to horrible and catastrophic dimensions. Doomsday lurks beyond the meeting for which you are late, the sale that you might not make, the deadline you might miss. It's no longer just the sale or report that is on the line; it is YOU.

The thought that paralyzed Peter, the creative director, was not that his screenplay would be bad. "Hell," he told us, "if that was all that was involved, the damn thing would have been written already. It's the *consequences* of writing a bad screenplay that really petrify me. It would signify that I've been kidding myself about one of the most important things in my life—my ability as a writer. If my work was not well received, *it* wouldn't be a failure, *I* would."

The fear that caused Rachel, the nutritionist, to say yes to everything and everyone was based on the same imagined conclusion. "Every time I'm asked to do something I'm afraid to say no because I might not get called, asked to speak or to advise again. That might cause me to lose my standing in the industry. My credibility would suffer and I might even lose my job."

An insidious aspect of fear is that you are often not conscious of what you are afraid of. Yet your heart pounds so loudly it feels as if it were going to burst out of your chest; your concentration leaps from one thought to another and you are unable to focus on anything. The intensity of these symptoms indicate how catastrophic the consequences of failing appear to your unconscious.

Fear Warning Signals

When in the Panic Zone, you will try to bulldoze through your fear. In the Drone Zone, you will be immobilized by it. C Zone performers recognize when they are performing from fear rather than confidence. Knowing that the fear, if unchecked, will continue to grow and prevent them from performing in the C Zone, they stop and confront this mental block.

As potentially devastating as fear can be to confidence and performance, you can learn, as Type C performers have, to be in control of yourself in the face of it. The first step is to recognize the warning signals which indicate that fear is affecting your performance. Just as there are signals on the dashboard of your car to indicate trouble, we all have a set of inner signals to alert us that fear is taking charge. The quicker you become aware of these "warning signals," the faster you can initiate action that will take you back to your C Zone.

Mental Warning Signals: Self-Talk

We all talk to ourselves continually. "Don't forget to do this." "Why did I do that?" "If only I . . ." "What if?" When we are afraid or worried, these inner conversations, called "self-talk," reflect fear and lack of confidence. This negative self-talk can be used as a warning signal.

The self-talk that warned me of a potential vicious cycle while writing this book was: "You're not working fast enough. You'll never finish on time." The self-talk that caused Rachel to panic was: "I should be available; I'd better make the time."

Recognizing Self-Talk

You don't need to wait until you are scared or in a vicious cycle to uncover your negative self-talk. Listing some of your own warning signals now will make them easier to recognize when the pressure is on.

Situation (example): Late for an appointment.
Self-Talk
"They're going to be really angry."
"They're not going to trust me. They'll think I'm a flake. They will never believe me."

"Dammit, why didn't I leave earlier?"

Now list your own examples and self-talk.

Body Talk: Physical Warning Signals

When Rachel is feeling overscheduled and then even more is asked of her, she says, her insides feel like they are racing. "My forehead and palms sweat. I have trouble catching my breath. I'm doing everything at fast forward."

Peter, when sitting at his desk to write his screenplay, has an almost opposite response. "No matter what time it is I feel sleepy. I find myself staring out the window, yawning and dreaming. And I just don't have any energy."

"Body talk," your physical and behavioral responses when under pressure, is another type of warning signal indicating that a vicious cycle has begun.

Recognizing Body Talk

Below are some typical body-talk warning signals. Check the ones that you experience when under pressure. Add some of your own that aren't listed.

> pain in the neck
> headache
> tightness in shoulders and chest
> shortness of breath
> clenched jaw
> tight stomach
> heart beating rapidly
> lower back pain
> dizziness
> dry mouth
> tapping feet, pencils, fingers

catching your breath
sighing
shaky knees
procrastination
losing temper
feeling speedy
feeling "wired"
pacing the halls

Substitution Rarely Works

A common and understandable response when you catch your negative self-talk is to tell yourself to think positively. But using positive self-talk in an attempt to change negative self-talk is fruitless. Your positive and negative self-talk will only argue with each other.

"Relax, you're going to be great in this interview. You've got all the qualifications."

"Yeah, but what if someone else is more qualified or they like them better?"

"Don't sweat it. Take it easy. You're terrific. Just relax."

"How can I relax? If I don't get this job . . ."

If you do pay attention to one of these voices it will be the one you believe. And if you really believed the positive self-talk you wouldn't have such a difficult job convincing yourself to think positively.

Stop!

If a warning signal on your car indicates trouble, ignoring it and continuing down the freeway is foolhardy and can exacerbate the problem. Pulling off the road and stopping gives you the time to assess the situation and figure out a next step.

The first thing to do once you have recognized your

own warning signal is to **Stop!** Take a few deep, slow breaths. Hold each breath for a count of three and exhale slowly. Just taking a few deep breaths will help you calm down and regain some of your lost composure. "When my heart is pounding, I make myself breathe in slowly, hold it, and breathe out slowly," says actress Jessica Tandy. "After a while the heart stops pumping so fast and I can go on."[10]

Stopping prevents you from getting deeper into the Drone Zone or the Panic Zone. It stops a vicious cycle. It gives you some distance from your fear, automatically increases your control and is a first step back to your C Zone.

Confronting Fear

"You gain strength, courage, and confidence by every experience in which you really stop to look fear in the face," said Eleanor Roosevelt."[11]

Stopping provides the breather needed to reevaluate the situation. It is now time to confront your fear to find out what is really going on—to do a reality check.

A reality check won't change the actual difficulty of a situation. It won't turn a mountain into a molehill. It will help you see what is really there. Fear makes a molehill seem like a mountain. A reality check will help you to see it for the molehill that it is. This more accurate appraisal will automatically diminish your fear and improve your performance under pressure.

The following four reality checks are methods for accurately assessing pressure situations.

Reality Check 1: Measuring the Difficulty

There was always a point in an Inner Skiing Week when the skiers thought I had taken them to a slope that was too difficult. When I would ask them how steep they thought the slope was, their fear would exaggerate the steepness and their answers would range from 50 to 70 degrees. If that were true, the slope would have been as steep as the face of El Capitan. I would then ask one of the skiers to do a reality check and measure the angle of the slope with his ski poles. He would invariably find that "it's only about 20 to 25 degrees." The sigh of relief would be audible. Their fear would turn to enthusiasm and they would start down the mountain without me. Seeing how steep the slope *actually was* as compared to *what fear had caused them to imagine* helped them to feel more confident and ski in the C Zone.

The fear that you won't get everything done can distort your perception and make your inner list seem twice as long and twice as hard as it really is. And you end up in a frenzy in the Panic Zone or paralyzed in the Drone Zone having undercut your normal effectiveness.

To get a look at what you *really* have to do, move the list from inside your head to outside, on a piece of paper or a board. Physically looking at it helps you see more clearly and evaluate it better than your fear-fogged imagination ever can. This type of reality-check list will help you calm down, evaluate the situation more accurately and focus your attention on what you are doing rather than on the self-talk about what still has to be done.

In some situations, like the ski slope and the "to do" list, a reality check can quantify or measure the actual difficulty. "Mountains" of paper, for instance, can be quickly sorted through to see how much *really* has to be done.

Messages can be counted to see how many phone calls *really* have to be made. Sales dollars can be totaled to see how much more you *actually* have to make in order to come in over quota.

Reality Check 2: Rating the Difficulty

Another effective technique for doing a reality check is mentally rating the difficulty. This method has proven reliable in sports, in medicine and in business for assessing and monitoring tension, pain and stress levels.

When the mind is asked to rate something, for instance on a scale of 1–10, it breaks through distortions created by fear and becomes analytical and objective. I have seen any number of people literally petrified by their catastrophic expectations of what *might* happen if they take a risk. Yet when asked to rate the difficulty of the task, on a scale of 1–10, they become extremely rational. It's as if at these times they do a mental flip from the emotional right hemisphere of the brain to the more analytical and rational left hemisphere, and shift automatically from the Panic Zone or the Drone Zone to the C Zone. The examples below and later in the chapter illustrate how to use ratings to assess a situation.

Reality Check 3: Rating Your Ability—Bringing the Past into the Present

Harold W. was in charge of writing promotion brochures for a fashion accessory manufacturer. Although he had a great deal of experience he became very anxious whenever he started a new brochure. He'd procrastinate almost to the deadline and then have to drive himself all the harder.

"When I sit down to write, all I can think about is that maybe I won't come up with a fresh idea and I clutch."

I asked him to rate the difficulty of the brochure on which he was currently working, on a scale of 1–10.

"It seems like an eleven," he joked. "Seriously, it's like I'm going to the gallows every time I sit down and think about the problem. All I want to do is run."

"Have you ever done a job that seemed this difficult before?" I asked, encouraging him to use the past to evaluate the present situation.

"Sure," he said. "Lots of them. They all seem this way."

I asked him to recall a particularly difficult one.

"It was the last one I did. We were introducing a quality line of accessories that was priced much higher than our competition. I had to position it at the top of the field, which was tough since the competition is very well established. But I came up with a unique approach and it got the best results of any piece I ever did."

"Great," I said. "Now remember the final piece, how it looked and the results it got. What conclusion about your ability would you draw from that experience?"

He looked around, a little embarrassed, and said, "I'm good when it comes to thinking up new ways of selling products."

"O.K., keeping that past success in mind, think about the new brochure you are working on. How would you rate the difficulty of this current piece?"

"It's about an eight." He smiled and, already looking more confident, added, "But that's a challenge I can handle!"

When you are in the clutches of fear you lose perspective. You think of past failures and future horrors. You forget that you have often been in similar situations and performed well. The actual difficulty of a situation and your ability to handle it can often be evaluated by looking through your memory bank for similar past experiences and making a comparison.

Remembering past successes helps increase your Type C confidence and start a vital cycle. Even when doing something new there will always be aspects that are familiar. You may have never written a year-end report, but you probably have done many monthly reviews. You may never have spoken to 500 people, but you have given many speeches to smaller audiences. There is always some experience from which to gauge the difficulty. Having a positive reality base, grounding yourself in what you *do know* and *have done,* helps you to reexperience your C Zone confidence and control.

Peter Thigpen, the president of Levi Strauss's U.S. operations, told us that he keeps a "victory log." "Small victories that I refer to when I'm feeling frustrated. I look at it to remind myself of my track record and my progress. I find it's a big help in relieving frustration and doubt and increasing my confidence."

But What If . . .

You will usually find, as Harold did, that the situation isn't nearly as difficult as you thought and the consequences are not catastrophic. But a reality check may indicate that the situation is more than you can handle: the mountain *is* a mountain. In these cases, just having stopped to do the reality check will have given you a little distance from your fear so that you can consider C Zone options which you were too panicked to notice before. You can ask for more help, reset a quota, reschedule a meeting or deadline.

Even though the situation is no less difficult, the reality check calms you down. Once out of the grip of fear, you'll naturally handle the problem from your C Zone.

Reality Check 4: Imagining the Worst

"Before taking any risk I always ask myself, 'What is the worst thing that can happen?' " Jo Fasciona, a vice-president for Pacific Telephone, told us. "Once I get a realistic idea of what that is, I decide whether I can live with these consequences or not. If I can, I go ahead and do it."

Many people resist confronting their catastrophic expectations. The possibilities seem so awful that they block them out and avoid thinking about them. This compounds the situation. Behind the curtain of fear, imagination invents all sorts of stories which, if unchallenged, will block C Zone performance and general well-being.

It is important to confront your catastrophic expectations. Unexamined prospects of disaster will keep you from performing in your C Zone. First, check the likelihood of your expectations *really* happening (on a scale of 1–10, will I *really* be fired if I am late?). You will usually find out your expectations are exaggerated. Once you have a realistic sense of what the outcome will be, you will no longer be controlled by fear. And you will be more confident, able to plot a C Zone course of action.

"Every time I start to think about expanding my business I stop. The consequences of failing seem so scary that I don't want to know about them." Ann B., a successful building contractor, was describing how she felt stuck for the past three years, and unable even to begin planning an expansion.

"What's the worst thing that could happen if you failed?"

"I'm afraid I'll make some terrible mistakes and go bankrupt. If that happened I'd probably lose everything I have—my equipment, my trucks and maybe even my house, to say nothing of my reputation. Ugh! I don't even want to think about it!"

"How realistic is all that, on a scale of one to ten, with ten being certain that you'll go bankrupt?"

She stopped for a moment to reflect. "I never thought of it that way before. It's probably only a four or at the very most a five." Her whole body relaxed as she said those numbers. "That's not as bad as I thought, certainly not the debtors' prison I pictured myself going to a minute ago. Actually," she continued, looking more confident and resolved, "even if I did fail I know I'd dust myself off and begin again. I'm highly skilled. Some of my competitors would probably be delighted if I closed my shop and would love to hire me."

The reality check helped Ann to see that the potential consequence of failing, although serious, wasn't nearly as catastrophic as she had scared herself into thinking. This realization broke the vicious cycle and allowed her to assess the situation realistically. Ann then felt confident enough to begin the planning process for a business expansion.

Dr. Charles Garfield, in his research on peak performers, found that most high-performing executives worked out a "catastrophic expectations report" either in their minds or in writing before taking a major risk. "They set out the worst that could possibly happen and decided whether they could possibly live with that outcome. If they could, they moved ahead confidently. Other executives," said Garfield, "didn't go through that process, and when taking a risk, tended to be hampered by a sense of impending doom."[12]

The Reality Check Eject Button

The relief, energy and renewed confidence you feel after doing a reality check become imprinted in your mind. Your mind knows a good thing! With practice you often won't even have to answer the question posed by your reality check. Simply asking it becomes like pushing an eject button that distances you from your fear and catapults you out of a vicious cycle and into your C Zone.

At a follow-up session Ann B. told us, "Whenever I notice I'm feeling panicked and in over my head I stop for a second and take a deep breath. Then I ask myself what's the worst thing that can happen? I no longer have to answer the question. Just asking it seems to short-circuit my panic. I immediately feel a sense of relief and can get on with what I want to do."

Being Fearlessly Foolish

The key to overcoming fear and increasing confidence is not to think positively but to think realistically. A reality check is very different from positive thinking. Thinking positively can actually have negative results, depending upon how you use it.

Convincing yourself that the sale you are about to pitch or the report you have to complete will be a cinch, when it actually won't be, will be detrimental to your performance. False confidence can cause you to underestimate the difficulty of a situation and overestimate your ability. The result is that you won't prepare as much, or as well, for the situation. You won't be as careful or diligent in what you say and do and you'll perform even worse than if you were scared.

Thinking positively but not realistically can cause you

to overcommit or overchallenge yourself. You end up like a beginning skier who, not knowing enough to be afraid, tries to ski an advanced slope. Because of his unrealistic confidence he has gotten himself in over his head.

From Anxiety to Action

You'll usually find, after doing a reality check, that a situation that appeared overwhelming will now seem challenging and possible. This shift in perception will change your attitude. You'll feel less anxious and tense, more confident and in control. The vicious cycle will have been broken and you'll move naturally into the C Zone ready for action.

Increasing Confidence—Overcoming Fear

1. Select a high-pressure situation in which you'd like to feel more confident and be more effective.

2. What is your confidence level on a scale of 1–10?

3. List your WARNING SIGNALS. Consider both self-talk and body talk.

Upon recognizing these signals remember to . . .

STOP!!!

BREATHE . . .

Take three deep breaths. Hold each breath at the top for a count of three and exhale slowly.

Reality Check

I. Rating the Difficulty of the Situation

1. If possible, quantify the situation. How much really has to be done.

2. On a scale of 1–10, how difficult is this situation?

3. Have you ever had a similar past experience? How difficult was it, on a scale of 1–10?

4. Based on your past experience, re-rate the difficulty of the present situation, on a scale of 1–10.

II: Rating the Consequences

1. What is your catastrophic expectation?

2. Based on everything you know about yourself and the situation, how realistic is that, on a scale of 1–10, with 10 being definite?

3. If your answer is 6 or less, answer question number 5.

4. If your answer to no. 2 is more than 6, what plans can you make to prepare for such an eventuality?

5. What is your confidence level now on a scale of 1–10?

CHAPTER SEVEN

Increasing Control: Type C Action

When we're afraid, as we have seen, we often respond inappropriately. Our distorted perception either immobilizes us, as it did Peter in the last chapter, and we end up in the Drone Zone. Or we go into fast forward, as Rachel did when hit with the requests she couldn't say no to, and end up in the Panic Zone.

Once a fear-generated vicious cycle has been broken with a reality check, you need to act. Taking appropriate action is the key to staying in your C Zone.

Everybody acts. We are all busy doing something. But there is one basic difference between the way you act when you're in the Panic Zone or the Drone Zone and the way you act when you're in the C Zone. That difference is control. Type C's know that in every situation there are elements that they can control and some they can't. Focusing attention and acting on what they can control maximizes their performance and effectiveness. Panic Zoners and Drone Zoners concentrate on factors outside their control, waste time and energy and become frustrated, disappointed and unsuccessful.

Picking up the phone, John T., vice-president of a large manufacturing company, learned that the report he needed for an important meeting would be late. When the researcher asked John if his secretary could help collate the report, he hit the ceiling. Pounding his fist on the desk, he yelled, "You'd better get that job done fast or there's going to be hell to pay, and do your own damn collating!"

John raged over something that was out of his control: a report that would not be done on time no matter how angry he got. His fit of temper alienated everyone. As with other Panic Zoners who fly off the handle, John's anger made it that much more difficult to get people to support his projects in the future.

It was 3 A.M. and Adam L. couldn't sleep. He was to give a presentation to a prospective client early the next morning. He had heard rumors that his competitor had an innovative new product and he worried over what he could do about it and what would happen to his expected promotion if he didn't get this account.

Adam's worries about making the sale were fruitless and frustrating. Whether the client would buy or not would be decided by factors that, at 3 A.M., were beyond his control. Nevertheless, he tossed and turned all night and arrived at this important meeting looking the worse for wear. He felt dull and tired, and his presentation lacked the spark and crispness that had always been his hallmark.

Kim L., who had fifteen years' experience managing video equipment stores, wanted to open a business that rented VCR equipment and tapes. She had the financial backing to make her dreams a reality. But she feared that the current market might flatten out and she would be left with a lot of useless inventory. She was also afraid that some competitor would start outspending her on advertising or undersell her. These fears loomed so large in her mind that they prevented her from acting on her idea.

Focusing on the unpredictable and uncontrollable marketplace kept Kim in the Drone Zone. As she "went through the motions" in a job that was no longer challenging and rewarding, she reinforced a vicious cycle of inertia and ennui.

Each of these people, dwelling on factors that were essentially out of their control, ended up either in the Panic Zone or the Drone Zone.

Controlling a Slump

Minnesota Twins outfielder Roger Ward was in a slump, hitting .226, when Coach Karl Kuehl asked him what he would be concentrating on in the game that night.

"I want to get a couple of hits and drive in a couple of runs," said Ward.

"A hitter doesn't have any control over whether he gets any hits or drives in runs," Kuehl told Ward. "There might not be runners on base [so there'd be no one to drive in]. A pitcher might make a perfect pitch. A fielder might make a great play. What a player can control is making sure he sees the ball well every time he goes up, making sure every swing he takes is a good one, making sure he knows the pitcher he is facing."[1]

Kuehl's advice pointed out the difference between those factors that were in Ward's control and those that weren't. Following Kuehl's advice and concentrating on what he could control, Ward went on a streak that saw him hit .326 with 22 home runs and 74 RBIs in the final ninety-six games of the season.

Ward's problem, common to many struggling to get out of a slump, was that he focused on factors *not* in his control. Every situation has a number of factors that will influence the outcome. Some of these are in your control and some aren't. Focusing on things that are beyond your control is frustrating, a waste of time and energy, and ensures Panic Zone or Drone Zone performance. Acting on those factors in your control guarantees C Zone effectiveness.

What You Can and Can't Control

Something is not in your control if it is externally influenced. As Kuehl points out, how well a pitcher pitches and whether a fielder makes a great play are out of your control.

Whether you will win a game is also out of your control. You can control how well *you* play, but that's only one of the variables that will decide the outcome. The other is how well your opponent plays. And that is out of your control. He or she may return your great shots with better ones.

In a sales presentation you can't control the client's needs, attitude, or response; what the competition may have offered; or the state of the economy—all of which play a significant part in determining whether a sale is made. You can control the information you have on some of these factors and how well you organize and present your material. But ultimately whether or not you make the sale is out of your control.

Not only can you not control another person's needs, attitudes or responses or how well he plays a game; you can't ultimately control anything he does. You may be able to influence his actions, but influence is often a long way from control.

Larry Wilson, the founder and chairman of Wilson Learning Corporation, a large management training company, clarified this distinction between controlling and influencing others in the following way. In a seminar we led together, he pointed his finger at the audience and said, "If this were a gun and I told nobody to move, would I be in control of you?"

"Damn right!" was the first reply.

"Seriously," Larry said. "Is this gun actually controlling your movements?"

"No, but it sure is a good influencer," someone shouted out.

"Right," Larry said, "and there is the difference. I can influence you in any number of ways, but ultimately I can't control what you do, even with this gun. Someone in the back could crawl out while I was looking the other way. Some other daring individual could throw something at me. Another person who didn't believe that I would shoot might call my bluff and just get out of her seat."

No matter how much you are in control of a situation, if the outcome involves another person's actions or decisions the result is out of your control.

Ultimately, as you can see, the only thing you can control is yourself—your own thoughts, feelings, attitudes and actions.

Great athletes seem to know this. They don't dwell on things that they can't control. Julius Erving up to 1982 had led his team to the National Basketball Association championship series three times, but lost each time. Yet he said of this quest, "I don't feel incomplete or inadequate in any way because I haven't won an NBA championship. I don't lie awake nights and think about it. I know I've given my best. The rest is out of my hands."[2]

When asked, after the 1983 World Series, if he would be

playing with the Phillies again the following year, forty-
one-year-old baseball great Pete Rose said that it's not up
to him whether he stays with Philadelphia and he never
worries about things that are out of his hands.

"You can't say you're going to win and then win," said
Peter Carruthers, who, with his sister, won a silver medal
in pairs skating at the '84 Winter Olympics. "Kitty and I
didn't come here to win a medal. We came to do the best
we could. We can't control how the other skaters skate.
We can't control how the judges mark us. All we can
control is ourselves and our skating."[3]

CAN-DO'S

Recognizing what they can and can't control, Type C
performers make the most of their time and energy by
focusing and acting on what they CAN DO. Type C actions
are CAN-DO's.

When I was behind in racquetball I used to try to break
through by yelling at myself: "Relax!" "Concentrate!"
"Get those next three points!" "Keep on your toes!" I
began noticing that some of these commands helped me
play better and some didn't.

The problem with much of the "good advice" I was
giving myself was that it didn't translate into action, so I
couldn't use it. What does "relax" mean? Which muscle?
How much? I don't want to be too relaxed.

"Concentrate!" On what?

"Get those three points!" How? What the hell do you
think I've been trying to do?

Although these commands were basically good ideas,
they were too vague to be of any help. They only served to
increase the pressure that was already fueling my Panic
Zone performance. The advice that did work—"Keep on
your toes," "Breathe out with every shot," "Keep moving

all the time"—led me to take action that was specific, constructive and in my control. And my performance improved immediately.

I applied these same parameters when giving speeches and presentations. I had tried to counter my tendency to talk too fast by telling myself to speak slowly. I even wrote notes at the top of the pages of a speech telling me: "Slow down!" But it didn't work. The problem was that "Slow down" wasn't specific enough. How slow? When? The instructions were too ambiguous. Besides, I was usually in so much of a hurry that I forgot to look at the note.

A CAN-DO that did work was to stop after each point I had underlined as important and make eye contact with three people in different parts of the room.

There are four simple characteristics—four C's—of a CAN-DO that will ensure effective Type C behavior in the most pressured situations.

Clearcut. CAN-DO's translate easily into specific action. Beware of commands that are too vague and general in nature, such as the ones I gave myself to relax and concentrate in the racquetball game or when I told myself to "slow down" during a talk.

Constructive. A CAN-DO is an action that will enable you to improve your performance and continue moving toward your goal. Making eye contact with three people when I gave a talk helped me to slow down, improve my contact with the audience and communicate better.

Current. A CAN-DO is an action that can be started immediately. It is the logical next step based on your past experience and ability level. Although it may relate to a future goal, it is something you CAN DO *now*. Getting on my toes and moving in the racquetball game was a CAN-DO that immediately improved my performance.

In your Control. A CAN-DO is an action over which you have direct control.

Increasing Control

CAN-DO's increase control of the uncontrollable. When you are planning for anything from a board meeting to meeting a deadline there are always elements that are in your control and those that are not. But you don't have to be a victim of factors that are out of your control. Identifying these factors is the first step to increasing your control. For every factor not in your control there will be something you CAN DO.

The remainder of this chapter teaches you how to recognize elements and situations that are essentially out of your control and to develop CAN-DO's for dealing with them.

After Fear: A CAN-DO

After Ann B., the contractor in the last chapter, used a reality check to break her fear, she made a list of CAN-DO's. She listed projects to bid on; additional equipment, personnel and services needed; made out a budget; saw a banker to determine whether expansion loans were available. These action steps started Ann on a C Zone vital cycle.

When you are afraid, your concentration is always on the future and what might happen if or when. When Ann thought about the possible consequences of expanding her business she became immobilized, too scared even to begin planning. Acting on the CAN-DO shifted her attention from the future, which was out of her control, to the present, which was in her control. This shift from the future to the present, from thinking about what she couldn't do to doing what she could, moved her from the immobility of the Drone Zone to the positive action of the C Zone.

A CAN-DO is empowering. It starts the ball rolling in the right direction and builds C Zone momentum, one CAN-DO leading to another. This Type C action increases your sense of control and self-confidence.

With CAN-DO's, you always win in the long run. If one action turns out to be an error in judgment, the Type C learns from the mistake and uses it to develop new CAN-DO's.

CAN-DO'S to Realize Your Goals

"I don't want to think about it," said Tamara McKinney about winning the World Cup in skiing. "I got into trouble last month [she fell in three races] because I was thinking about it and putting too much pressure on myself. All I want to do is concentrate on each race."[4] A few months later, McKinney became the first American woman to win the World Cup.

Putting all of your attention on something you want to accomplish in the future, rather than what you CAN DO now, takes you out of your C Zone. Because they are influenced by other people, the economy, competition, politics or any number of other external factors, goals are out of your control.

Focusing exclusively on a goal can also be discouraging. The further off the goal, the harder it will seem. Many joggers, before they even run a hundred yards, are thinking about how far they *still* have to go. "Ugh! Three more miles!" This thought makes their body feel heavy and sluggish. The three miles seem more like three hundred and the C Zone at least that far away.

Additionally, a path leading to a long-range goal will appear laden with obstacles. "When I am calling on a client," said William T., an insurance salesman, "and find out that a proposal and final decision have to go through many channels, I get discouraged. The sale seems too far off. Too much can go wrong and probably will. It seems a waste of my time to follow through."

The more you are focused on the future, the more likely you are to make mistakes in the present. If you are skiing and concentrating on a difficult turn ten feet ahead, you can easily lose your balance on the turn you are on.

The Drone Zone is filled with people like Kim, the video store manager, and William T., the insurance salesman, who have unfulfilled goals and unactualized dreams. Focusing exclusively on the future paralyzes these types. Rather than worry about the future, they need to develop a series of CAN-DO's that will get them into action.

This doesn't mean you shouldn't have a goal. Type C performers have clear, well-defined goals. But once they set their goals, they focus their attention on what they CAN DO now to achieve them.

A CAN-DO is like a step carved into the face of a steep mountain. While reaching the top represents a major challenge, or the realization of a dream, each step is taken in the present with confidence. These Type C actions are realistic, achievable and measurable and lead to the attainment of long-term goals.

CAN-DO's ensure success. Success increases confidence. A vital cycle has been started! "Building success into your goals is critical," says Charles Lynch. "It's important to see success. Once you have succeeded you can build on that. You can take another notch up the ladder. These initially small successes build a sense of accomplishment."

What You CAN DO about What Has Been Done

We've all been in situations in which we've said or done something we later regretted. To make things worse, long after such an incident we feel guilty and worry about the repercussions. If we don't blame ourselves, we blame someone else. Worry, blame and guilt take your attention out of the present and away from what you CAN DO.

Despite the fact that three of his superstars defected to another league and a number of his star players had debilitating injuries, Don Shula, the coach of the Miami Dolphins, led his team into more Super Bowls than any other coach in the National Football League. "I don't dwell on things I can't control," he says. "What's past is past. It's gone. It's yesterday."[5]

You can't do anything to change the past. Past events, like future goals, are out of your control. But you can learn from the past and, on the basis of that information, act in the present, focusing on what you CAN DO.

"The Past is gone, the Future not yet. All there is is the *now,*" said Fritz Perls, the father of Gestalt therapy.[6] CAN-DO's bring both the past and the future into the present. Type C's learn from past experience, act in the present and move toward future goals.

Anticipation vs. Worry

Although you can't control the future, anticipating it is something you CAN DO now. But there is a big difference between anticipating the future and worrying about it. The worrier, a Panic Zoner or a Drone Zoner, imagines all the nightmarish possibilities that *might* occur and feels out of control. Firmly planted in a vicious cycle, the worrier is either too panicked or too paralyzed to act effectively, and therefore continues to worry.

There are several CAN-DO's that Type C's use to anticipate the future. They speculate, role-play and preview in the present to develop a repertoire of CAN-DO strategies for responding to anything that might occur.

Speculating is thinking about any eventualities that might happen and developing responses for them. President John F. Kennedy was a master at speculation as a means of preparing for his meetings with the press. "Before every presidential news conference, Kennedy and a half dozen of us would sit down and go over every possible question that he might be asked. When he went to a news conference, he had been briefed to the gills. So he almost never got a surprise question," reported Dean Rusk, Kennedy's Secretary of State.[7]

Role Playing is "walking a mile in the other person's moccasins" and imagining how it feels. One chief executive officer told us that before a stockholders' meeting he goes down to the auditorium and sits in several different seats. "I imagine myself as the person who will be sitting there, and see what I would be feeling, thinking and wanting if I were them. What questions would I have? What would be my concerns? I then figure out how best to respond. I prepare for all important meetings by trying to fully understand the concerns of everyone there."

"Lyndon Johnson had a genius for working with a problem from the point of view of the other fellow," according to Dean Rusk. "He could put himself in the other fellow's shoes. It gave him a considerable understanding of the nature of the problem," Rusk says. "This was one of the attributes that made Johnson a fantastic persuader."[8]

Previewing is visualizing yourself in a future situation, picturing all the things that might come up and imagining what you CAN DO to respond to them. Fran Tarkenton, who passed for more yardage than any other quarterback in NFL history, used previewing to prepare for his upcoming games. "On this week, for example, I must think of Pittsburgh [the opponent] and nothing else. I must see that Steeler defense in my dreams, every one of them, knowing their names, bodies, moves. I must be able to tell who is chasing me by the sound of the footsteps, and which way to turn to evade him, for every man has his weakness. I must see those linebackers eyeing me as they backtrack into pass coverage, know their relative speed and effectiveness, know just how many steps each one will take on specific defensive calls so that I can find the right hole at the right time. By Friday, I'm running whole blocks of plays in my head . . . I'm trying to visualize every game situation, every defense they're going to throw at me. I tell myself, 'What will I do on their five-yard line and it's third and goal to go, and our passing game hasn't gone too well and their line looks like a wall and we're six points behind?' "[9] Whatever happened in a game was, to Tarkenton, little surprise. He had already pictured a response for almost every possibility.

What You CAN DO about the Unexpected

Inevitably, something that you hadn't planned for occurs. About four years ago I was caught in traffic on one of the famous Los Angeles freeways, which at that moment resembled a giant parking lot. Nothing was moving. I was on my way to an important meeting and I knew this jam would make me late—if I got there at all. I was frantic and started banging on the horn and steering wheel, looking to jump lanes, take an emergency exit or go up on the grass. But there was no way out.

Then, in a moment of C Zone clarity, I asked myself, "What can I do about the traffic?"

"Nothing," was my response. "It's out of my control." And with that realization came an incredible sigh of relief. My whole body relaxed. It was as if a great weight had been lifted from my shoulders. There was nothing I could do about getting the traffic to move.

"O.K.," I said to myself, "what is a CAN-DO for this mess?"

I chose to rehearse my presentation and to take the time to speculate about the other people who would be at the meeting and each of their specific agendas.

After I felt I had done enough, I turned on some music and did some people watching. When I arrived, I was relaxed and better prepared. And my mood helped to smooth any irritation about my lateness.

Even when the unexpected occurs and appears out of your control, there's always something you CAN DO that will keep you in your C Zone.

What You CAN DO about Anger

Whether it is an associate who is late, a machine that has broken down or a traffic jam, getting angry means that you feel out of control of the situation. Anger is caused by focusing on what you can't control. The more you focus on the CAN'T-DO, the angrier and more out of control you feel.

While John T., the manufacturing vice-president, ranted and raged about what couldn't be done, he couldn't think clearly enough to determine what could. He could have assessed how late the report actually would be. He could have called the people coming to the meeting, explained the situation and perhaps rescheduled it. He could have developed an alternative plan for summarizing and presenting the material that was in the research.

The key to breaking the hold of anger is to switch your thoughts from what you can't control to what you CAN. Instead of expending your energy raging about a broken machine or a late colleague, you can use the CAN-DO to stay in the C Zone, where you can control and direct your energy constructively instead of blowing it off in a cloud of steam.

The Silent CAN-DO

The first time Tim Gallwey, my co-author of *Inner Skiing,* and I were conducting a program together, Tim was asked a question by a ski instructor who obviously had an ax to grind. Tim stood there thinking for what must have been at least two minutes. I was worried and wanted to help out, but he waved me away. Finally he came up with an answer that was perfect. When I asked him later about the pause, he said, "It was a good question and I didn't know the answer. I needed time to think about it."

Often we think we should have an immediate answer when asked a difficult question. We are afraid to stop and think for fear of looking foolish or seeming stupid. We then respond from the Panic Zone or the Drone Zone, too quickly, with a reply that is not well thought out. This can undermine your effectiveness in any situation.

Type C's, acting from CAN-DO to CAN-DO, know that there are many moments when the next step to take or response to make is not immediately clear. The most effective CAN-DO at that point is to stop and think.

"There's a difference between a speech and a spiel," Coca-Cola president Don Keough says. "A lot of speakers are afraid to think while they're speaking. I think it's an enormous tribute to an audience to let them know that you are not only talking to them, but that you're thinking right in front of them. When I sense that a speaker is thinking out loud with me, I feel that he's willing to be vulnerable, willing to let the thoughts that are flowing into his head right at the moment be out there for me to evaluate. I think he's being respectful to me."[10]

Control Check and CAN-DO Plan

In retrospect we usually know the CAN-DO's that would have kept us in the C Zone. In a follow-up seminar, salesman Adam L. commented on his behavior. "I should have known I couldn't do anything about a competitor's new product. The best thing I could have done was to get a good night's sleep. I'd have been rested and in my C Zone for the presentation and would have maintained a good working relationship with the client whether I made the sale or not. It's so obvious now. Why didn't I think about it then?"

Under pressure we often forget what we know and overlook the obvious. The C Zone strategy when under pressure is to STOP!; take a few deep breaths and assess the situation, this time, by doing a control check and CAN-DO plan:

Control Check and CAN-DO Plan

1. List all the factors in the situation that will influence the outcome, include everything from the weather and the economy to your client's mood.

2. Review the list and mark a 'C' next to each factor that is in your control and an 'NC' next to each factor that is not in your control.

3. For each 'C' list the CAN-DO's.

4. For each 'NC' list the CAN-DO's that will increase your control in that situation.

5. Prioritizing the CAN-DO's from both your 'C' and 'NC' lists can become the basis for an effective action plan.

CAN-DO: Concentrated Action

The more focused you are on a CAN-DO, the more your concentration intensifies, until you enter into what golfer Tony Jacklin calls "a cocoon of concentration," where nothing distracts you.[11]

Billie Jean King blocks everything from her focus except one CAN-DO. "I concentrate only on the ball in relationship to the face of my racket, which is a full-time job, since no two balls ever come over the net the same way."[12]

Former All-Pro quarterback John Brodie says, "A player's effectiveness is directly related to his ability to be right there, doing that thing in the moment. He can't be worrying about the past or future or the crowd or some other extraneous event." And in those intense moments of concentration, Brodie claims that "time seems to slow way down, in an uncanny way, as if everyone were moving in slow motion. It seems as if I had all the time in the world to watch the receivers run their patterns, and yet I know the defensive line is coming at me as fast as ever. I know perfectly well how hard and fast those guys are coming and yet, the whole thing seems like a movie or a dance in slow motion."[13]

The intense concentration that comes from focusing on what you CAN DO will enable you to perform in your C Zone, at your peak in the most high-pressure situations.

CHAPTER EIGHT

Programming Yourself for the C Zone

When under pressure most of us are usually only aware of thoughts—"Uh-oh! I'm going to blow it"—or physical sensations, such as sweaty palms or a pounding heart. But it is our unconscious mental images of how we will perform that create our self-talk, feelings and the resulting physiological responses. "Feedforward" is the term that Stanford neurophysiologist Karl Pribram uses to describe these images of achievement and misachievement that precede and affect all of our actions.

Your mind works in pictures. These mental images shape your attitude and guide your behavior. The late Italian psychiatrist Roberto Assagioli wrote in *The Act of Will* that "images and mental pictures . . . tend to produce the physical conditions and the external acts that correspond to them."[1]

An image in the mind fires the same neural connections in the autonomic nervous system as an actual experience.

As a result, research has shown, the body can't distinguish between an actual experience and a clearly held and deeply imprinted image. Therefore visualizing yourself performing in your C Zone is perceived by your mind as real. This mental rehearsal serves as an effective tool for imprinting Type C performance patterns, developing a Type C attitude and increasing the frequency of your C Zone behavior.

Maximizing Performance

The importance of mental imagery for enhancing performance was pointed out in an experiment done by the Russian Olympic team. Russian and Eastern European athletes are far more sophisticated in mental training than are their counterparts in the West. Dr. Gregory Raipport, former psychiatrist for the Russian Olympic team, told us, "With us it is a science." Prior to the winter Olympic Games of 1976 the Russians divided athletes into four groups with different ratios of mental to physical training.

	% PHYSICAL TRAINING	% MENTAL TRAINING
Group A	100	0
Group B	75	25
Group C	50	50
Group D	25	75

The improvement in performance for each group was then measured over time. The group that showed the best incremental improvement was Group D, those athletes who spent 75 percent of their time practicing mentally and 25 percent physically.

There have been many experiments indicating the positive effects of visualization. George Sheehan in his book, *On Running,* wrote of a test study done by Canadian physicians in which they divided post-coronary patients into two groups. One group was given a program of daily jogging and exercise. The other only did mental imagery. "They imagined themselves jogging or pictured themselves in a beautiful meadow filling their lungs with wonderful fresh air and feeling the oxygen going through the whole body reaching the heart."

After a year the results were identical for both groups. Weight and body fat were down. There was an increase in grip strength and EKG tracings. Blood pressure was lowered and adrenaline production by the body was lowered.

Equally dramatic are the results of a research study involving three groups of students chosen at random, shooting basketball foul shots. One group physically practiced foul shots for thirty minutes a day. The second group did nothing. The third group visualized themselves shooting foul shots for twenty minutes a day. At the end of twenty days the first group which had practiced every day improved 24 percent. The second group which had done nothing showed no improvement. The third group which had only visualized themselves shooting fouls improved 23 percent![2]

Jack Nicklaus attributes 10 percent of his success to his setup, 40 percent to his stance and swing and 50 percent to the mental imagery he uses before he takes each stroke.[3]

Nicklaus is only one of the many world-class athletes who use visualization, the technique for creating and controlling mental images, to prepare for pressure situations. Baseball great Joe Morgan visualizes himself swinging a bat "even when I'm in the bathtub."[4] Track star Mary Decker has imagined herself running the final lap of the 3,000-meter run in the 1984 Olympics more times than she can count. And Phil and Steve Mahre, the gold and silver medalists in the slalom at the 1984 Olympics, were seen on international television visualizing their runs as they waited in the starting line. The list of world-class athletes who use visualization to maximize performance would sound like a Who's Who of sporting greats. It includes Bill Russell, Fran Tarkenton, Billie Jean King, Jim Brown, Arnold Schwarzenegger, Lisa Lyon, Jean-Claude Killy, Jane Frederick, Steve Carlton and Bill Walton, to name just a few.

Improving Mental Performance

Visualization works for more than just sports. It is extremely effective for increasing confidence and preparing for any type of situation, mental or physical. Type C's in business, politics, medicine, law and the arts whom we interviewed all used mental imagery to prepare for pressure situations.

Time Inc.'s Dick Munroe told us that as part of his preparation for an important speech he imagines the whole environment. "I will see in my mind what it looks like, who will be there, how they will be seated and how I want to come across."

"Windmilling" is what Bettina Parker calls her process of mental rehearsal. When Ms. Parker, the president of a large international marketing and consulting firm, is working on an important project, she visualizes it all in her head and rehearses it until it plays out perfectly. She'll often practice like this for days prior to a meeting to make sure she has everything worked out just right.[5]

This chapter will teach you different ways to use visualization to program yourself for C Zone performance. Imaging yourself as a Type C will help to imprint C Zone behavior and make it your automatic response to any pressure situation.

Re-viewing 1: Your Personal Highlight Film

Tom McMurphy, a former small-college All-American basketball player who is now a successful insurance salesman, told us that whenever he had a big game coming up he would review in his mind his "personal highlight film." "I would visualize the tough games I had played really well in. Watching these old tapes gave me confidence and got me psyched up.

"I do the same thing now in selling," McMurphy said. "When I have to make an important presentation and am feeling nervous about it, I rerun one of my selling highlight films. I visualize the last time I made a successful presentation. If I have time I might even run several of them. Running these old tapes not only gives me confidence but reminds me of some of the good moves I've made."

A recent research study indicated the effectiveness of a personal highlight film for improving performance. An actual videotape focusing on a professional basketball player's great moves—his slam dunks, great passes, perfect assists—was prepared. The player watched the tape twenty times over a thirty-game period. His point production for that period increased 41 percent! His steals per game increased 60 percent![6]

Visualizing your own inner highlight film and watching it before you go into pressure situations will help to increase your confidence and program you for C Zone performance. Most of us already have enough material to make up our own highlight film. Over 90 percent of the people who attend our management seminars report previous successes in the same types of situation that presently cause them stress.

Visualizing a Type C experience creates a chain reaction. When you image a past success you imprint that Type C experience in your mind. This increases your confidence that you CAN DO it again and initiates a vital cycle.

Re-viewing 2: Getting That Old Feeling

"I'm not tough enough when I need to be," Ian, a literary agent, told me. "I work out great deals for my clients on paper but I'm terrible at face-to-face negotiations. I never want to ruffle any feathers or make anyone angry. When things get tough I have a tendency to get nice. And because I'm too easy I'm not as effective as I could be."

"How would you like to be?" I asked him.

"Tough," he said, and then added, "and independent, not concerned with what people think of me."

Ian couldn't remember ever having been tough and independent in a negotiation session. So I asked him if he had performed with these qualities at any other time in his life.

He thought for a minute and then said, "The picture that came to my mind was when I was on the tennis team in college. I was great at the net. My volleys were real hard and sometimes aimed right at my opponent. I wasn't worried about being liked. I wanted to win. And in my senior year I made the semifinals in the regional championships. I was smart and tough as a player. That's exactly the way I'd like to be for my clients."

I had Ian re-view scenes in his mind from his tennis experience and focus on his attitude. Images create feelings. Re-viewing an old mental tape will help you to reexperience the feeling you had at that time. As Ian reran his old tennis tapes his jaw became more firm and set, his mouth tightened and his face took on a more serious look. He even sat straighter. In a fifteen-minute visualization exercise he had transformed into a formidable, determined and intimidating-looking individual.

Feelings and attitudes are transferable. If you have expressed them in one area of your life, they are available to be expressed in other areas as well. Ian now had a highlight film which he could use to prepare himself for future negotiating sessions.

Laurie K., a successful manager of rock music groups, used the same technique to motivate herself for tasks that she didn't like to do. She loved playing squash and would often play a couple of games before going to the office. This would give her a lot of energy and enthusiasm, which she'd then automatically bring to the job. When she didn't have time to play she'd take five minutes or so imagining herself playing. "I'll always remember a tight game, one in which I played real well. I'll run through the great points I made. After doing this mental exercise I'll feel powerful and full of energy. Making those phone calls I had dreaded would then seem easy."

Making Your Highlight Film

The first step to creating your personal highlight film is to recall a relevant Type C experience. Select either the same type of situation or one in which you have experienced, as Ian did, the attitude you desire. Then re-view that past situation. Play it back in your mind in as much detail as possible. Re-view the actions, feelings and thoughts that helped you to be successful. Look for the little things you did, the gestures you used, the routines you set up, how you moved, your tone of voice.

Run your mental tape back to a point *before* the event and see how you psyched yourself up or calmed yourself down for it. Look at everything you did which might be helpful in this situation.

Then see yourself accomplishing your goal; shaking hands with the client who signed the contract; finishing the project; being applauded by an appreciative audience. Seeing yourself achieve a past goal will help you to reexperience the feeling of confidence, exhilaration and overall well-being that you had at that time.

Rerun your tape several times. Make the movie as real as possible. Picture where you were, who was there, even what you were wearing. Everything. The impact of this past Type C imagery on your present attitude and actions will increase in direct proportion to the clarity, detail and intensity of your imagery.

Bringing the Past into the Future

The next step is to transfer your past experience into the future. See yourself performing with the same Type C confidence, attitude and skills in the upcoming situation that you had in the past one. Project into the future. Visualize yourself thinking, feeling and acting in the C Zone with as much clarity and detail as possible. See the environment you will be in. Visualize yourself in action accomplishing your goal.

Previewing will increase your confidence. You are also automatically practicing and refining your skills when using this mental rehearsal technique. Previewing also serves to make the real situation seem more familiar when you are actually in it.

Previewing the Perfect Performance

"I never hit a shot, not even in practice," says Jack Nicklaus, "without having a very sharp, in-focus picture of it in my mind. It's like a color movie. First I see the ball where I want it to finish, nice and white and sitting up high on the bright green grass. Then the scene quickly changes and I see the ball going there: its path, trajectory and shape, even its behavior on landing. Then there is sort of a fade-out, and the next scene shows me making the kind of swing that will turn the previous images into reality."[7]

Many top performers, like Nicklaus, have Type C images already imprinted in their mind. Their Type C behavior has been repeatedly grooved. When visualizing, they simply project those images into the future situation without needing to re-view a past experience.

Scott T., the president of a marketing research company, was called upon to testify at a highly publicized trial involving one of his firm's clients. Although all he had to do was present research data, which he did regularly at client meetings, he was worried about how he would come across. He was concerned that his nervousness might be construed as evasion and that he would lose his credibility. He also felt a lot of pressure because the client for whom he was testifying was one of the firm's biggest.

Scott prepared himself by previewing. He imagined himself calmly walking into the courtroom and sitting down. He saw all the details in the room: where he sat, with whom, the judge, the two sets of attorneys, his clients, the spectators . . . He then visualized himself being called to the witness stand and played out the scene, seeing himself as a Type C responding to questions and presenting his research findings. Then he saw himself leaving the witness stand feeling confident and self-assured.

After several mental run-throughs he was relaxed and feeling much more positive. He later said that testifying had been a snap. "I felt like I had been through the whole thing before. Funny, though, the scenario that I rehearsed in my head was a lot tougher than the real one."

Type C Ideal Models

Bill Russell, the great center for the Boston Celtics who revolutionized defensive play in basketball, used visualization as a teenager to practice new moves while traveling from one game to another on the high school bus. "I was in my own private basketball laboratory, making mental blueprints for myself. It was effortless, the movies I saw in my head seemed to have their own projector, and whenever I closed my eyes it would run. . . . As our tour rolled through a string of cities . . . I was not only learning the game but adding to it. Every day turned into an adventure."[8]

Russell used an ideal model in his imagery to learn new skills and refine his moves. "I was working on learning how to take an offensive rebound and move quickly to the hoop. It's a fairly simple play for any big man in basketball, but I didn't execute it well and McKelvey [another player] did. Since I had an accurate version of his technique in my head I started playing with the image, running back the picture several times and each time inserting a part of me for McKelvey. Finally I saw myself making the whole move, and I ran this over and over, too. When I went into the game I grabbed an offensive rebound and put it in the basket just the way McKelvey did. It seemed natural, almost as if I were just stepping into the film."[9]

Having a Type C ideal model provides you with mental pictures which act as a guide for refining your own C Zone behavior. It can be used to develop a specific attitude like aggressiveness or receptiveness. You can emulate the open-mindedness with which someone responds to suggestions, the authoritativeness with which someone runs a meeting, the determination of Marie Curie, the inspiration of Martin Luther King, the competitiveness of Bill Russell.

JFK and I

When I began speaking to large audiences I was intimidated and nervous, and I often came off flat. At about this time I happened to view a film of John Kennedy giving his inaugural address. I was very moved by his presence and made it a point to review many of his speeches. I began developing a mental tape of him, seeing him in my mind's eye making a major speech. My mental picture of him focused on his power, authority and presence. Gradually I began replacing his image with mine until I could see myself as an authoritative speaker.

Ideal Modeling

To increase your C Zone behavior by using an ideal model, first choose an individual who expresses those characteristics you want to develop, as I did with JFK. Then create a mental tape of examples of these characteristics so that you can see them clearly in your mind. Gradually edit yourself into the tape until you can see yourself performing with the same assurance as your Type C model. With practice, this visualized Type C behavior will become a natural response when you are in the real situation.

Turning Failure to Success

Several years ago the governor of a large midwestern state told us he had changed his relations with the press by using this technique. "When I was first elected," he told us, "my relations with the press were very poor. I couldn't figure it out since I knew that my stand on most of the issues was popular. I also knew I was well informed, so that couldn't have been the problem. I was puzzled and concerned. My wife suggested my problem might have less to do with what I said than how I said it. Her comment got me to review one of my press conferences on video-tape. Watching it, I realized that she was right. I was standing with my arms crossed, my mouth was tight and I was hunched over. I looked very unfriendly, defensive and angry. I didn't even like me.

"For my next meeting, in addition to preparing my remarks and information," the governor continued, "I visualized how I wanted to look, in terms of my posture, the expression on my face and my movements. I also saw myself being more open and friendly and not as defen-sive. From that day on my relations with the press im-proved dramatically."

If videotape is not available you have your own source of video feedback—your mental movies. Everything you ever do is imprinted there. You can retrieve this informa-tion and re-view it to see how you did and to correct mistakes.

"If I had a play that I muffed on the court, I'd go over it repeatedly in my head, searching for details I'd missed," said Bill Russell. "It was like working on a jigsaw puzzle; one piece in the completed picture was imperfect and I had to find out what it was."[10]

The Type C approach to mistakes is to "catch 'em and correct 'em." Errors that aren't found tend to be re-peated. The best time for this re-viewing process is as soon as possible after the situation occurs.

The advantage of finding errors is that they can be corrected. Jean-Claude Killy, the former Olympic triple gold medal winner, used visualization, as many ski racers do, to prepare for his races. Prior to one race, it is said, Killy saw himself in his mental movie falling at a gate, something he rarely did. He reviewed the race in his mind and once again saw himself fall at the same gate. But this time he discovered why. He had been skiing into that gate at too sharp an angle. He then reran the mental movie, seeing himself take a less extreme angle into that gate. It worked perfectly. He reran it several more times in his mind to get it perfect. The next day he took the less extreme line at that gate and won the race.

Visualization can be used to correct mistakes, break habits and turn failure to success. Your mental movie can be edited, replacing the error with pictures of yourself performing as a Type C. After editing your C Zone performance into the tape, re-view it often to imprint the changes in your mind. Your Type C version is now foremost in your memory and will become your automatic response to that situation.

Guidelines for Making Your Own Movies

Although "imagery" is the term most generally used for mental movies, not everyone actually sees pictures. Mental imagery is auditory, kinesthetic and olfactory as well as visual. Some people are more inclined or oriented toward one of these senses than the others. Many people who use visualization very effectively never actually "see" their mental movies. Some get a "feel" for the picture or "sense" it. A good friend of mine "listens" to it.

The following guidelines will help to make your Type C mental movies more effective. Although we use the word "see" in these guidelines, it is meant to encompass any of the other ways you may experience your imagery.

1. **Relaxation.** You can't take a good picture if your camera isn't steady. Similarly, visualization is most effective if your mind is steady. The more relaxed and free of distraction you are when visualizing, the clearer your mental

pictures will be and the images will imprint more deeply. (Several relaxation techniques are discussed in the next chapter.)

2. Make Them Real. The effectiveness of your imagery is largely dependent upon how specific and detailed it is. Your mental movie should be as close to the real thing as possible. If you are rehearsing for a meeting, for instance, start by seeing something familiar and build upon it until you can see the whole scene fully. Take your time. Keep adding details until you have a sense of being there. Then see yourself going through the same step-by-step sequence that you would in the actual situation.

3. Your Own Role in the Movie. There are two roles you can play in your movie. You can play the observer and watch yourself perform. This is helpful when you are reviewing a past experience or using an ideal model, as it allows you a more objective look at your performance.

You can also play the participant—be the player in your own movie and feel yourself perform. Being the subject of your own movie is particularly useful when you are rehearsing for an upcoming situation.

To get the greatest benefit from your Type C mental movies, play both these roles. See how it looks from the outside, and then feel and practice it from the inside.

4. Experience It Fully. A friend told me that when Olympic triple gold medal winner Jean-Claude Killy visualized a ski race he could hear the crowd, feel the wind and the cold on his face, feel his legs pumping and the edges of his skis carving through the snow. Mary Decker actually experiences the feeling of coming off the final turn in the 3,000-meter run, lifting her knees and arms, extending her stride, sprinting fast. In the basketball foul-shooting experiment involving visualization, those who did best reported feeling the ball in their hands, feeling their knees bending as they shot and hearing the swish as the ball went through the net.

Experiencing your mental movie as fully as you can imprints C Zone behavior images most effectively.

Triggers: Bringing Your Type C Movies to Life

You can increase the effectiveness of your Type C movie by using a trigger—a specific action transferred from your imagery into the real situation. A trigger serves as an "on" switch, automatically re-creating, in an actual situation, the Type C behavior you rehearsed in your mental movie.

Bill Buckner, the first baseman of the Chicago Cubs, demonstrates the effectiveness of a trigger. When Buckner comes up to hit he will lightly tap the plate with his bat. That tap serves as a trigger for the imagery he has practiced in which he sees himself being more selective at the plate and hitting only those pitches he wants to hit. The tap on the plate reminds Buckner, at an unconscious level, of the imagery and automatically brings about its results. Prior to his imagery sessions, Buckner had been having a poor season. Directly after, he raised his batting average 30 points and was voted the National League's Player of the Month. Buckner felt that as a result of this imagery he became more confident, relaxed and selective at the plate.[11]

When you are developing your Type C movie, select some action—like taking a drink of water, polishing your glasses, turning your ring, holding your hands a certain way—that can be transferred to the real situation. Rerun that part of the movie. Practice the trigger physically as you are visualizing yourself doing it. These triggers will automatically bring that Type C imagery to the forefront of your mind when in the real situation. Your Type C images will then guide your behavior in the situation.

Visualization is a powerful tool you can carry with you anywhere. You can practice it in your office, commuting, waiting on line, in elevators, before you go to bed and on vacations. Rerunning a well-edited Type C performance tape is exciting and exhilarating. It increases your confidence and prepares you to perform in the C Zone.

CHAPTER NINE

Conditioning: Getting in Shape for the C Zone

The Body-Mind Connection

The health benefits that accrue from physical conditioning are well known. Less well known is the effect that physical conditioning has on attitude and mental performance. "Body, Mind and Soul are inextricably woven together," says cardiologist Paul Dudley White, "and whatever helps or hurts one of these three . . . helps or hurts the other two."[1]

Most of the Type C's I interviewed stressed the importance of being in good physical condition. "My physical conditioning is critical to my work. It bothers me mentally if I'm not physically fit," Dick Munroe told us.

Physician Linda Weinreb, who maintains a private practice, makes rounds at a local hospital and works in a free clinic, discussing the effects of conditioning on her attitude, says, "When I don't exercise I'm lethargic and disengaged. I get irritable much more easily and tire more quickly. When I exercise regularly I'm more vital and positive. I have a feeling of fullness. I'm more present for my patients and my work is much better."

Your physical condition plays an important part in determining the performance zone in which you will play. A body that is tight and overstressed will limit your effectiveness and productivity in any activity. It may even break down and need continual attention.

The body and mind are inextricably interrelated. A poorly conditioned body causes mental as well as physical fatigue, preventing you from operating in your C Zone for long periods of time. Poor conditioning is detrimental to your attitude, vision and enthusiasm. It undermines your mental processes, decreasing your ability to concentrate and think clearly.

Good physical conditioning increases the likelihood of performing in the C Zone. Just as mental attitude affects physical performance, physical conditioning affects mental attitude. "Getting to the top demands strength, endurance and energy whether it is the top of a mountain or the top of your profession," Tom Simpson told us. "Physical and mental strength are directly related. People who tire easily or burn out fast won't make it. You've got to be in good physical condition to perform at your peak."

The degree to which you keep your body in good condition will influence your ability to operate in your C Zone. But being a Type C isn't dependent upon having a perfect body or being in shape for a marathon. Some Type C's do have terrific bodies and some do run marathons. Others are more sedentary. Some Type C's are physically limited or disabled.

Type C conditioning means having your body in the condition necessary to help you meet and exceed the demands of whatever you want to do. Being in good physical condition helps you to feel better and think clearer, to experience more vitality and aliveness and to have more energy, endurance and strength so that you can perform at your C Zone best more often.

Four Components of Fitness

There are four basic components of a physical conditioning program that will get you in shape for the C Zone.

1. Aerobic training
2. Flexibility
3. Strength building
4. R & R—relaxation and revitalization

Type C Conditioning 1: Aerobics

If you were to limit yourself to only one conditioning activity, aerobics would be the one to choose.

"Aerobics," writes Dr. Kenneth Cooper, author of *Aerobics,* "increases the maximum amount of oxygen that the body can process within a given time. This is called your aerobic capacity. Aerobic training strengthens your heart and lungs, and develops a good vascular system."[2]

Attitude and professional performance are enhanced by aerobic exercise in many ways.

1. **Increased Energy.** "Now that I exercise regularly I have more energy to handle the ups and downs of my job and my life and to find solutions to problems that I previously would have been too tired to even think about," Myrtle Harris, former infant and children's wear buyer for a major national chain, who is now the president of a senior citizens residential community, told us. "I work more efficiently, accomplish more in less time and don't tire as easily."

2. Mental Alertness. Type C's applaud the value of physical fitness for enhancing mental prowess. "Being in good shape gives me more energy so I can work faster and longer. I feel more alert, mentally sharp. My thinking is clearer," says Larry Gershman, president of M-G-M/UA Television Group and a former professional basketball player.

"My brain is much sharper after a run and I can deal with a lot more stress," Levi Strauss's Peter Thigpen told us.

3. Self-confidence. Research has shown that people who are in good physical condition tend to have a more positive self-image. The results of a study at Purdue University showed that self-confidence and self-assurance increase as physical conditioning improves. Participants in the study also became more outgoing, more involved with others and more emotionally stable.

4. Creativity and Imagination. "Methinks that the moment my legs begin to move, my thoughts begin to flow," said Thoreau. The Purdue study also confirmed Thoreau's insight that physical conditioning spurs the imagination. It's common knowledge that people often get creative breakthroughs and insights while on a run or a long walk.

5. Stress Reduction. Dr. Cooper writes that exercise increases your ability both "to deal with specific stress situations that occur during the course of each ordinary day" and "to relieve yourself of stress at the end of an especially pressure-filled day so that you're more relaxed and energized and ready to work or play, even into the evening hours."[3]

6. Improved Appearance. You look more vital, vibrant and alive. You have more color in your complexion, more muscle tone and less fat.

7. Feeling of Well-being. Physical exercise helps you to feel better mentally, physically and spiritually. Many psy-

chologists now prescribe running to combat depression.
An added benefit is that exercise generates an abundance
of endorphins, which are associated with states of well-
being and euphoria.

The physiological benefits of aerobic exercise are well
known and equally positive:

- Lower blood pressure.
- Lower resting heart rate: the heart, because it is
  stronger, does not have to work as hard to transport
  blood to the rest of the body.
- Increased cardiac output: the heart is better able to dis-
  tribute blood where needed under stress.
- Increased number of red blood cells: more oxygen can be
  carried per volume unit of blood.
- Increased elasticity of arteries.
- Lower triglyceride level.
- Decreased blood cholesterol; high-density cholesterol,
  which is more protective of blood vessels, is proportion-
  ately increased.
- Adrenaline secretions in response to emotional stress are
  lowered.
- Lactic acid is more efficiently eliminated from the muscles, decreasing fatigue and tension.
- Additional routes of blood supply are built up in the
  heart.

How Much and How Hard

Although running receives the most publicity, it is hardly
the only type of aerobic exercise. Any vigorous activity
done for an extended period of time fits into this category.
Walking, swimming, biking, aerobic dance, jumping rope,
cross-country skiing, roller skating, rowing and square
dancing, among other things, can all be done aerobically.

Aerobic exercise should be done so that the heart is working in what is called the "target zone." This is the level that is vigorous enough to strengthen but not overtax the heart and vascular system. To determine your target zone, subtract your age from 220 (the approximate maximum stroke rate of the heart). Your target zone is between 70 and 85 percent of that number. For example, if you are forty years old it would be:

$$220 - 40 = 180$$
$$85\% \text{ of } 180 = 156$$
$$70\% \text{ of } 180 = 126$$

Your target zone would then be between 156 and 126 beats per minute. You should exercise at this rate a minimum of *three times per week for twenty* minutes per session.

Starting Out

Many people after hearing that they have to exercise vigorously for at least twenty minutes a day three times a week are overwhelmed. They haven't exercised in years and feel they would be lucky to make it around the block. They're right! Exercising vigorously for twenty minutes a day three times a week is too much at first. So do what you CAN DO now. Begin slowly. You will probably get into your target zone quite easily at first. Some people who have not exercised for years will get into their target zone by just going out for a brisk walk. So don't overdo it. Your maximum benefit will come from staying in your target zone. Keep it fun. Make exercise an enjoyable experience, one that you want to do again.

If you are beginning an aerobic training program and are over the age of thirty-five or physically out of shape, it is wise to get a complete checkup, including a treadmill test.

Fatigue: Mental or Physical

Often after a busy day at work as I am getting ready to go for a run, my self-talk starts out first: "I'm too tired to run today, I think I'll take the day off." Sometimes it's true, my body needs a rest, and it is a good idea to take the day off.

Most often, though, it is my mind, which I have been exercising all day, that is tired. The only thing I have done with my body, besides sit, is to go out for lunch.

When I hear that familiar self-talk I do a reality check to see if I am experiencing physical or mental fatigue. I'll stand up and move around, even jog in place a little, to see how my body feels. With a little practice you'll be able to discriminate between mental and physical fatigue.

Heavy Blankets

In response to a question about the most difficult part of his strenuous early-morning workouts, John Akii-Bua, the winner of the 400-meter hurdles in the 1972 Olympics, replied, "The blankets." He explained that the blankets in his bed were so warm and comfortable that he had great difficulty lifting them to get out of bed.

If, when the alarm rings, you feel listless and your blankets feel too heavy, remind yourself why you want to exercise in the first place. Take a few minutes and visualize how wide awake, vital and full of energy you will feel after you exercise. If you have a specific goal you are shooting for—weighing ten pounds less, looking more attractive, being more energetic at work—visualize yourself accomplishing it.

Larry J. disliked running vehemently, but felt he had to run in order to eat desserts without gaining weight. We asked him to visualize himself eating his favorite dessert before he went for a run. He later reported, "I could actually see a sundae. It had coffee ice cream with lots of hot fudge, fresh whipped cream and nuts on it. I could even taste it! And no guilt or bad feelings while I ate it. I went a mile further than usual. It was great! I even pictured that sundae the whole time I ran."

Michelle also disliked exercise but loved the experience of power and control that came from a twenty-minute workout each morning. "I'd lie in bed and think about how I'd feel about myself and my ability to handle the day if I had exercised and if I hadn't. That always got me up. A day that I've begun by exercising is a day in which I feel more powerful and in control. I figure if I can get someone as recalcitrant as me out of a warm bed to exercise I can do anything!"

Beating Boredom

One of the more common complaints about aerobic exercise is that it is boring. But nothing is inherently boring. Boredom occurs when the mind is out of control and concentrating on what is not happening rather than what is.

Many Type C's use aerobic time to plan, problem-solve or review their day. A psychologist friend reviews her cases as she rides her bike. A director of training for a large corporation prepares his programs while running. An architect designs houses down to the most minute detail on his daily ten-mile run.

Other Type C's use their aerobics as an opportunity to get away from people and pressure and to unwind. They dream and fantasize, letting their minds take a breather while their bodies are working.

You can combine fantasy and reality by imagining yourself accomplishing goals you usually only dream about. Allow your imagination to run wild. Let yourself daydream. See yourself as famous, wealthy, the president of your company, having a beach house on the Riviera. Besides being fun and energizing, these fantasies can help you learn more about yourself and what you really want.

Back-Burnering

There is a creative process that often takes place during exercise. The conscious mind may not be focusing on work during your exercise but the unconscious is. It's as if there are two burners in the mind. The front burner coincides with the conscious mind, and the back burner, the unconscious. The mind doesn't just drop a problem or a project on which it has been working. It switches it from the front to the back burner.

Therefore, while you are exercising, your unconscious mind is still making connections, searching for answers, developing new perspectives. There actually seems to be a need for back-burner incubation in the creative process. This is the reason so many people solve problems and have insights while on a run, a walk, a ride or swimming laps.

Thomas Hoving, the former director of New York City's Metropolitan Museum of Art, who is now the publisher of *Connoisseur* magazine, told us that he gets some of his most creative ideas while on his daily bike ride.

Type C Conditioning 2: Flexibility

My introduction to stretching, which has had a very dramatic effect upon my life, was quite fortuitous. In my late twenties, after being extremely athletic for most of my life, I began having lower back pains. After several excruciating episodes I decided to see an orthopedist. He recommended an operation if I wanted to continue leading a physically active life.

A week and a half before the operation was scheduled I met an old friend and invited him to spend the weekend with me in the country. Early Saturday morning I found Chuck doing some strange-looking exercises, which he explained were yoga. Their purpose, he elaborated, was to increase the flexibility of the spine.

He offered to teach me some of the postures. I was skeptical, but the pain in my back was nagging, so I decided I had nothing to lose. He taught me some basic positions, whiche we practiced for about a half hour. I felt wonderful. I was very relaxed when we finished and yet full of energy. I practiced the postures several more times that weekend and my back felt better than it had in a long time. For the next week I did yoga for twenty minutes both before work and in the evening when I got home. My back felt so good I canceled the operation.

I have been practicing yoga as well as other forms of stretching every morning for the last fifteen years. My chronic lower back pain has never returned. My back is often stiff in the morning, but after ten to fifteen minutes of stretching it is loose and flexible, and I feel more energized.

Tension saps energy and enthusiasm. Stretching relaxes tense muscles and helps your body remain limber and resilient. It increases energy and range of movement and improves your general feeling of well-being.

Many Type C's use stretching exercises during the day to relieve tension and loosen tight muscles. "A few minutes of stretching and I feel fresh," Alyce C., the vice-president of sales for an equipment-leasing corporation, told us. "I am more energetic and alert and my body feels loose and relaxed."

Loosening Up

You can loosen up when feeling tense anytime and any-where, in your office, commuting, in a meeting, by increasing your tension! It is a natural tendency, when you feel tight, to try to stretch the tense area. But stretching pulls against the tension. Like a tightly coiled spring, a tight muscle will often just spring back to its original tense position after you stop stretching it. And if you pull too hard, if you strain rather than stretch, it will spring back even harder and you'll have a pulled muscle.

The best way to relax a tight muscle is to go *with* the tension—exaggerate it! If your tension feels like a 5, tighten further to an 8. Then SLOWLY let go as you exhale. The voluntary tension that you have added to the tight area releases the involuntary tension. Then when you let go the whole area will begin to relax. From that relaxed position you can stretch by moving slowly and easily. Remember, it's stretch, not strain. Doing this exercise five times starts the muscle moving, which breaks the tension and increases its flexibility.

Pain in the Neck

A common tense spot for people working under pressure is the neck, shoulders and upper back. To release tension in this area, exaggerate the tension in time with an inhale. SLOWLY tighten your shoulders and neck. Lift your shoulders as you tighten them and jut out your jaw. Hold the tension and your breath for a count of three. Then SLOWLY release the tension as you exhale. Do it five times nice and easy.

There are many good books on stretching. You can, as I often did when I was learning, take a yoga or stretching class. Most aerobics classes also include stretching. The great proliferation of fitness activities has resulted in the growth of sports medicine clinics. These clinics will teach you stretching exercises specially designed for your body and for your particular needs.

Type C Conditioning 3: Strength Building

"Just throwing around those weights made me feel stronger and more powerful," Joan G., a vice-president of a bank, told us. "This was important because I had always seen myself as weak. Lifting weights changed the image I had of myself. It actually helped me feel more comfortable and confident competing on the job. I feel I can hold my own with anyone now."

Building physical strength helps you to feel stronger mentally and perform in the C Zone. Harold W., a marketing executive who keeps three-, five- and ten-pound dumbbells in his office, told us that before he started exercising with weights he felt like the ninety-eight-pound weakling in the Charles Atlas ads. "But now I feel stronger, not just physically but mentally. Somehow," he said, "the physical strength translated to my psyche. I have more confidence now and feel personally more powerful. I have the courage I didn't have before to take the risks I need to."

Strong muscles do more than make you feel powerful. They provide support for the skeleton, resulting in less strain on your bones and ligaments. Building abdominal muscles, for instance, gives you more tone, helps you to look better and also reduces strain on your back.

There are many ways of building strength at home or in the office by doing push-ups or half push-ups, sit-ups and other calisthenics or lifting weights. You can buy a home gym or exerciser. There are also health clubs which will give you an individualized strength-building program for your whole body. If you don't stand around too long between exercise stations at the gym, these programs have an aerobic benefit as well as building strength and muscle tone.

Type C Conditioning 4:
R & R (Relaxation and Revitalization)

Typical Panic Zoners who work seventy- or eighty-hour weeks often brag, "My work is my life, I have no hobbies, my job is my only interest." They are actually working against themselves.

"I'm dead against workaholics," says Dick Munroe. "Working like that causes you to lose enthusiasm and vitality and inhibits creativity."

All high-performance systems need a rest cycle. Both mental muscles and physical muscles need rest in order to revitalize. Without it they become fatigued, lose power and efficiency and eventually burn out. Therefore, an essential part of a conditioning program is what we call R & R—relaxation and revitalization.

R & R periods can vary in time and intensity from a long vacation to a five-minute break in the midst of a pressure-filled day. They can be physically active or meditationally tranquil. The key aspect of R & R is to take a real mental and physical break from what you are doing.

Destressing

Stress is cumulative. It keeps building with each pressure event that takes place during the day. Let's say you start out the day at a base stress level of 3 (on a scale of 1–10). An angry phone call can jolt your stress up to a 6. After the situation has been handled your stress will decrease, but not to the level where it was before the phone call. It may now be a 4. A few more tense situations and your base stress level is a 6, and you're way out of the C Zone.

If you don't reduce your stress it will continue to build. By the time you leave the office your stress may be staggeringly high. You may be irritable and preoccupied. You might lose your temper and fly off the handle over the least little thing. Or you might try to drown out the day and everything else with alcohol. If this continues your base stress level the next day will be even higher. The Panic Zone or Drone Zone vicious cycle that develops is dangerous to both your health and your productivity.

An R & R break at the end of the day will decrease your stress. But when you have been engrossed in a problem or project it is difficult to simply stop thinking about it and relax. Diverting your attention is much more effective.

Many people find exercise to be a form of R & R. Physical exercise of any kind is a great way to bring closure to your workday and keep you in the C Zone. It will help to sweat out tension that has accumulated. Because it gets your blood moving and oxygenates your system, exercise also increases your energy level and revitalizes you.

Senator William Proxmire walks at the end of the day. "I can start off tired and weary after a long day in the Senate, with all kinds of frustration, feeling too tired to sleep and far too tired to walk. . . . After the first difficult quarter or half mile not only does my frustration ease . . . I feel more rested and fully alert."[4]

Dee Samuels, a partner in a prestigious San Francisco law firm, says, "I sometimes feel run-down at the end of the day. If I go for a run it dissipates those feelings and gives me energy."

But an R & R break doesn't have to be physically vigorous to get you back into the C Zone. The president of a major publishing house makes chairs. A well-known network television news reporter plays the piano for a half an hour at the end of the day to relax and unwind. A vice-president of a large brokerage firm loves to tinker with the engine of her car when she gets home from work. "It's like therapy," she told us. "I get so involved that I forget the troubles of the day. There's also a great feeling when I fix something."

It doesn't matter what you do to relieve your stress at the end of the day. The key to C Zone R & R is involvement in something that is satisfying and engrossing and takes your mind off the job. Although you may be sitting in your easy chair with your feet up, reading a detailed report in the evening after you have been working hard all day may increase your mental and physical fatigue. So might any activity that doesn't allow your mind to rest and revitalize.

Working Late

Because it decreases your stress and increases your energy, an end-of-the-day R & R break will help you become more productive if you do have to work late.

When I worked in advertising I played in a softball league between 6 and 8 P.M. After playing I would often return to the office. I found that after a ball game I had much more energy and was more creative and productive. On the other hand, when I hadn't taken an R & R break, and had either skipped dinner or had a quick bite at my desk, I tired much earlier. My enthusiasm and energy were lower and the quality of my work wasn't nearly as good.

Many people are very creative late at night. A senior partner in a Wall Street law firm told us that she does her most creative work between 10 P.M. and midnight. "It's quiet in the house. The phone isn't ringing and no one bothers me, so I can concentrate without distractions, and get a lot done. But ," she told us, "if I didn't take a break and relax after work I'd be too exhausted to do anything. This way I get two more productive hours and have still spent some quality time with my family."

Shifting Gears: Taking a Time-out

A well-known syndicated columnist told us that when he gets stuck writing he will stop and shift his attention. "I may do a menial task, some trashy reading which doesn't require a lot of heavy thinking, play some tennis or even go to a movie. It's too bad there are no showers at work. I get some of my best ideas there.

"I don't have any hard and fixed rules about what I should do at these times," he continued. "I know I have to take my mind off the article I'm writing. I've done as much as I can. My mind needs a rest. Invariably, either during or right after my break, I will get a flash—I don't know how else to describe it—that gives me some new insight or perspective."

When pressure becomes overwhelming, an athlete, or a team, takes a time-out to calm down and assess the situation. Pausing to relax and revitalize yourself in the middle of a pressure-filled day enables a Type C to perform for longer periods with less fatigue and loss of concentration. To realize the fullest benefits of these R & R breaks, it's important to "disconnect" mentally, as well as physically, from the pressure.

"I've been a golf nut ever since I can remember, so when my mind starts to race in all directions I take out my putter and a few balls and practice putting for a couple of minutes," Harvey K., a broadcasting executive, told us. "It takes all of my attention to get that ball into the cup. This little break relaxes me and I'm better able to concentrate when I get back to work."

In the middle of the day, when he feels tired, psychologist and author David Brandt will often sit back in his chair, put on earphones and listen to some electronic music. It so captivates him, he says, that for those moments he forgets the day. "The music relaxes me and gives me a lift, so that after five minutes or so I feel refreshed, energized and ready to go again. The earphones are great because they drown out everything else."

When he is overwhelmed with phone calls, copy changes and shortened deadlines, graphic designer Peter Bailey will stop and do a five-minute routine he learned while studying T'ai Chi. At the end of it, he says, "I feel like a new person, calmer and with a lot more energy."

Taking a Five-Minute Vacation

Joanna S., a marketing executive, uses visualization to help her relax in the middle of a hectic day. She closes her office door, stops her calls, sits back in her chair and takes a five-minute trip to her favorite beach in Hawaii. "I feel as if I am really there," she told us. "In my mind I see the colors of the ocean, the trees, the sand, the sky. I put as much detail as I can into the scene, which makes it seem more real. Sometimes I actually hear the ocean, feel the warm sand and the air on my face and even smell the sea. After a few minutes at the beach I feel renewed and full of energy. I feel like I can handle anything that comes up."

Beating the Blahs: Taking an Oxygen Break

The "blahs"—we all know what they are. Just before lunch you run out of steam. Around four o'clock you start feeling drowsy and unfocused. The cause of the 11 A.M.

and 4 P.M. "blahs" is a lack of oxygen. The combination of minimum physical activity and maximum stress results in shallow breathing, which reduces oxygen. We feel sluggish and concentration is difficult.

Often we'll take a coffee break at this time to get a needed energy boost. But coffee and/or sugar only work for a brief period of time and ultimately keep you from performing in the C Zone. The chemical reactions in the body brought about by sugar or caffeine result in a sharp drop in energy after an hour or so.

You can get the energy boost needed to stay in the C Zone without the detrimental or addictive effects of caffeine and sugar by oxygenating your system.

Doing moderate exercise, something that gets you breathing a little more heavily but not sweating, will give you a burst of energy. I do some push-ups and half sit-ups when I feel sluggish at work. You can take a quick walk around the block. We know an executive who will walk up a few flights of stairs, which, he says, "gets my heart pumping and gives me some energy as well as a little time out of my office and away from the phone and people."

Doing the top half of a jumping jack is especially effective. Moving your arms up and down rapidly for two or three minutes increases your heart rate, which oxygenates your system and invigorates you. One executive we interviewed had a rowing machine in his office, another a stationary bike. When they felt logy, they would take a little energy break.

When I taught I always preferred a schedule of morning classes. The students were more mentally alert then and so was I. In the afternoon they were lethargic and fuzzy in their thinking and just generally less present. One semester I had to schedule two afternoon classes but remedied the situation by starting each class with five minutes of vigorous exercise. The change was amazing!

Everyone was much more awake and alert. Our thinking was clearer and crisper and we were all more enthusiastic.

Catching Your Breath: A Mini Time-out

Oxygen breaks can help you relax as well as give you a boost of energy. Breathing rapidly and vigorously oxygenates your system and gets you going when you are feeling sluggish. Deep, slow breathing, on the other hand, helps you relax and calm down when you are tense and speeding.

Many Type C performers use deep-breathing exercises to relax when under pressure. Paul Annacone, who was the number 2 player on the University of Tennessee tennis team, said that at one time if he had played a few points sloppily, he would get mad at himself and fume through the break between every other game. Now, he says, he will "sit down in the chair, drape a towel over my head, relax my head and shoulders, close my eyes and then take deep breaths. . . . If I'm just thinking about that [the breathing], I can't be thinking of anything else. So my mind is taken away from the tennis and the competitive atmosphere. I feel refreshed and energized, but not overexcited, when I go back to play."[5]

Annacone's national collegiate ranking, after he started taking this R & R break, went from forty-second in 1982 to second in 1983!

And who will forget Arthur Ashe meditating between games in the finals at Wimbledon in 1975 when he beat Jimmy Connors.

Deep-Breathing Exercises

You can practice a deep-breathing technique now. Start by noticing the pace and depth of your breathing. How fast are you breathing? How far down in your body can you feel your breath reaching? Now gradually begin to slow your breathing and breathe more deeply.

Counting along with your breathing keeps your attention on your breath rather than on tension-producing thoughts. Inhale slowly to the count of four. Hold your breath for a two count. Then exhale slowly and easily to the count of six.

Tension/Release

An effective means of easing tension is the loosening-up method we discussed earlier. Briefly, further tighten an already tense muscle and then slowly release it. Tensing and releasing a tight muscle starts it moving, which breaks the tension, and automatically begins to relax it. Coordinate these movements with your breath. Tighten the tense muscle on an inhale. Hold it in that position as you hold your breath. Then slowly release the muscle in time to an exhale.

To relax totally from head to toe, work your way up your body, tensing and releasing each muscle group in time with your breathing. Try it now. Begin at the bottom. Tense your feet as you inhale for a count of four—curl your toes, tighten your arch, tense your whole foot. Hold your feet tense as you hold your breath for a count of two. Then slowly relax them as you exhale for a count of six. Gradually work your way up your body, tensing and releasing each major muscle group—calves, thighs, buttocks, stomach, back, arms, shoulders, face—in time with your breath and counting: in for four . . . hold for two . . . out for six . . .

Relaxation Triggers

The effect of relaxation exercises is cumulative. The more you practice them, the easier it becomes to relax and stay in the C Zone in pressure situations. If you initially take ten to fifteen minutes to do a deep-breathing or tension/release exercise, the body's sense memory will begin to remember the effects of the exercise. You will soon be able to bring about the same result by tensing and releasing only one muscle group.

Dr. Julie Anthony, a clinical psychologist and former world-ranked tennis player who was on the staff of the Philadelphia Flyers hockey team in 1981–82, taught relaxation exercises to the players in which "the player sits in a relaxed position and progressively tenses and relaxes all the major muscles in his body." Regarding the triggering effect of these exercises, she said, "Practicing this twice a day for fifteen minutes, he eventually can take a few breaths, tense and relax a few muscles and feel his entire body relax. In the game, if the score is close and he is waiting to go in, he can use this technique to keep himself from getting too tight. Or if he has just been involved in a brawl, he can skate around for a few seconds, use the relaxation technique and then be able to play effectively."[6]

Bill Kennedy, the national sales manager for a management training corporation, explained how he uses the triggering effect of these relaxation exercises. "In a tense meeting I will hold my hands behind my back, or under the desk, and tighten and loosen my fist a few times in time with my breathing. It really helps me to relax and stay calm under pressure."

Vacations

Type C's recognize the value of vacations. Getting away from the pressure-filled work environment for a couple of days or weeks is mentally, physically and spiritually revitalizing.

When Arch McGill gets away to ski or play tennis, he

does nothing related to business. "A diversion is necessary," says McGill. "It really recharges me."

"After a vacation I'm excited about getting back to work," Tony Morgan told us. "I'm enthusiastic and energized. My perceptions are sharper. I see things much clearer than before I left."

It's quite common to see old problems with new eyes (and a Type C attitude) after spending a week skiing, scuba diving, white-water rafting or just relaxing on a beach.

Conditioning for the C Zone

A finely tuned body is an invaluable asset to Type C behavior. The physical qualities of flexibility, strength, resilience, energy and endurance that you develop from a conditioning program automatically begin to transfer to the mental, enabling you to overcome many obstacles to performing in the C Zone.

You will think more clearly and be able to concentrate for longer periods of time when you are in good physical condition. Your confidence is heightened and your enthusiasm increased. You are more vital and have the energy and courage to push past previous limits and stay in the C Zone for longer periods of time.

CHAPTER TEN

Believing in Yourself

Beyond Tips and Techniques

Each technique discussed in this book is designed to help develop one of your Type C characteristics so that you can perform in the C Zone more often. The reality check, for instance, increases your confidence by teaching you how to overcome fear. It helps transform anxiety into Type C action. CAN-DO's and control checks increase control and make your actions more effective. Visualization helps to prepare you mentally for a pressure situation and to imprint Type C behavior.

There is no one best technique for everyone. There's no one specific order in which to use these methods. Depending upon where you are in your life, which performance zone you frequent and which Type C characteristic you need to develop, some of these techniques will be more meaningful to you and more relevant than others. If, for instance, you are having trouble making a commitment, daydreaming would be a good place to start. If you are racing around overstressed in the Panic Zone, taking a five-minute "vacation" break in the middle of your workday will calm you down, increase your self-control and help you to get back to your C Zone. Because situations are constantly changing, and you are continually growing, if you reread this book in six months other techniques will emerge as valuable to practice.

Although these techniques help overcome the mental obstacles that prevent C Zone performance, this book is about more than a variety of techniques. A technique isn't magic. It can't create something out of nothing. What it can do is facilitate the emergence of what is already there.

A technique is like a key. It opens a door and allows you to see what is behind it. The techniques in this book allow you to experience what is already inside you. They help overcome the fears, doubts and other negative attitudes that keep your natural ability and inherent potential locked up. These techniques open the door to your innate Type C behavior. They allow you to experience how well you already know how to perform when mental obstacles are overcome. But your Type C ability is already there. If it weren't, no technique would work. You'd turn the key and nothing would happen.

Understanding that you already are a Type C and have the innate ability to be a peak performer is far more important than any technique. Knowing that you are a C helps you to identify with your potential rather than with your problems. This shift in your self-concept changes the way you experience and express yourself and how you relate to the world. It enables you to act from a position of strength rather than weakness, to feel more powerful, confident and in control of yourself in any situation and to continue to grow, change and transcend previous limits.

Each limit exceeded, each boundary crossed, verifies

that most limits are indeed self-imposed, that your C Zone potential and possibilities are far greater than you ever imagined, that you are capable of far more than you ever thought.

There are no adequate external measurements for Type C behavior. There are the internal measurements of joy, vitality and well-being. There is the knowledge that throughout your life you will continue to exceed your own limits and break your own records.

The Fourth C: Courage

There is no status quo for the Type C. Security lies in knowing, experiencing and trusting your Type C nature. In the C Zone you are continually learning, growing and confronting new challenges. It is not surprising that the last C is courage. It takes courage to change, to confront your fears, to break familiar habits and to stick with what you believe, even though it may not always be easy or comfortable.

It takes courage to commit to your own deepest desires, to play your own game and "go for it" in whatever you choose. Ultimately it takes courage to live life to the fullest of your ability, to be the most you can in whatever you do.

As you close the book, recall a past Type C episode. See it in your mind's eye. Feel it. Experience the power that is in you. Remind yourself that you are already a Type C; that your C Zone potential is always there, waiting to be expressed in everything you do, wherever you go.

If you would like to receive information on C Zone tapes, programs and seminars, write:

The C Zone
P.O. Box 5052
Mill Valley, CA
94942

NOTES

INTRODUCTION

1. Dr. Ken Dychtwald, "Anxious Executive," *Forum*, June 1981.

2. Dr. Kenneth Pelletier, *Wholistic Medicine: From Stress to Optimal Health* (Delacorte, Delta/Doubleday, 1979).

3. San Francisco *Chronicle*, March 18, 1982.

4. *Winner*, No. 1 (Scholastic, Inc., 1982).

5. *San Francisco Magazine*, September 1982.

6. Transcript of Sales Competency Report, Forum Corporation, December 1981.

CHAPTER ONE

1. Albert Szent-Györgyi, "The Drive in Living Matter to Perfect Itself," *Synthesis Journal*, Vol. I, No. 1 (1974).

CHAPTER TWO

1. "L.A. Needed a Pat on Its Back," *Sports Illustrated*, June 21, 1982.

2. Dr. Kenneth Pelletier, *Wholistic Medicine: From Stress to Optimal Health* (Delacorte, Delta/Doubleday, 1979).

3. Ibid.

4. San Francisco *Chronicle*, September 26, 1982.

CHAPTER FOUR

1. Billie Jean King, *Billie Jean.* (Viking, 1982).
2. San Francisco *Chronicle,* January 8, 1982.
3. "An Image in Sharper Focus," *Sports Illustrated,* May 31, 1982.
4. *New Age Magazine,* January 1978.
5. "He Took It All and Would Not Fall," *Sports Illustrated,* December 6, 1982.

CHAPTER FIVE

1. *Women's Sports,* June 1983.
2. Ibid.
3. Napoleon Hill, *Think and Grow Rich* (Fawcett, 1960).
4. *The Wall Street Journal,* January 21, 1983.
5. Thomas J. Peters and Robert H. Waterman, *In Search of Excellence* (Harper & Row, 1982).
6. "The Reluctant Champion," *Success,* December 1983.
7. *Sports Illustrated,* February 20, 1984.
8. *Women's Sports,* June 1983.
9. *New Age Magazine,* January 1978.

CHAPTER SIX

1. *Sports Illustrated,* July 5, 1983.
2. San Francisco *Chronicle,* March 1, 1984.
3. Thomas J. Peters and Robert H. Waterman, *In Search of Excellence* (Harper & Row, 1982).
4. *Ms.* magazine, October 1983.
5. *Sports Illustrated,* September 12, 1982.
6. Sandy Linver, *Speak and Get Results* (Simon & Schuster, 1983).
7. *Observations from the Treadmill* (O.F.T. Union, 1976).
8. "An Image in Sharper Focus," *Sports Illustrated,* May 31, 1982.
9. Ibid.
10. *Decker Communications Report,* July–August 1982.
11. Eleanor Roosevelt, *You Learn by Living,* 1960, as quoted in *The Quotable Woman,* ed. Elaine Partnow (Doubleday/Anchor Press, 1978).
12. *The Wall Street Journal,* January 21, 1983.

CHAPTER SEVEN

1. "The Slump: Who Has the Cure?" *Sport Magazine,* August 1983.
2. *Sports Illustrated,* June 21, 1983.
3. New York *Times,* February 19, 1984.
4. San Francisco *Chronicle,* March 11, 1983.

5. Los Angeles *Times,* January 22, 1983.

6. Joel Fagan and Irma Lee Shepherd, *Gestalt Therapy Now* (Science and Behavior Books, 1970).

7. Sandy Linver, *Speak and Get Results* (Simon & Schuster, 1983).

8. Ibid.

9. Michael Murphy, *The Psychic Side of Sports* (Addison-Wesley, 1978).

10. Linver, *Speak and Get Results.*

11. Murphy, *The Psychic Side of Sports.*

12. Ibid.

13. Ibid.

CHAPTER EIGHT

1. Roberto Assagioli, *The Act of Will* (Viking, 1971).

2. Mike Samuels, M.D., and Nancy Samuels, *Seeing with the Mind's Eye* (Random House, 1975), pp. 166, 167.

3. Michael Murphy, *The Psychic Side of Sports* (Addison-Wesley, 1978).

4. *The Pacific Sun,* May 1983.

5. Grace Lichtenstein, *Machisma, Women and Daring* (Doubleday, 1981).

6. *Women's Sports,* September 1983.

7. Murphy, *The Psychic Side of Sports.*

8. Bill Russell, *Second Wind: The Memoir of an Opinionated Man* (Ballantine, 1979).

9. Ibid.

10. Ibid.

11. *Sports Illustrated,* September 13, 1982.

CHAPTER NINE

1. Philip Goldberg, *Executive Health* (McGraw-Hill, 1978).

2. Ibid.

3. Ibid.

4. Michael Murphy, *The Psychic Side of Sports* (Addison-Wesley, 1978).

5. Emily Greenspan, "Conditioning Athletes' Minds," New York *Times Magazine,* August 28, 1983.

6. Ibid.